Picture
Patchwork

15 Charted Patterns for Novelty Quilts

Jo Ann Lepore

Landauer Publishing

Picture Patchwork

Landauer Publishing, www.landauerpub.com, is an imprint of Fox Chapel Publishing Company, Inc.

Project Team
Acquisitions Editor: Amelia Johanson
Managing Editor: Gretchen Bacon
Editor: Sherry Vitolo
Designer: Wendy Reynolds
Indexer: Jean Bissell

ISBN 978-1-63981-057-4

The Cataloging-in-Publication Data is on file with the Library of Congress.

To learn more about the other great books from Fox Chapel Publishing, or to find a retailer near you, call toll-free 800-457-9112, send mail to 903 Square Street, Mount Joy, PA 17552, or visit us at www.FoxChapelPublishing.com.

We are always looking for talented authors. To submit an idea, please send a brief inquiry to acquisitions@foxchapelpublishing.com.

Note to Professional Copy Services:
The publisher grants you permission to make up to six copies of any patterns in this book for any customer who purchased this book and states the copies are for personal use.

Printed in China
First printing

This book has been published with the intent to provide accurate and authoritative information in regard to the subject matter within. While every precaution has been taken in the preparation of this book, the author and publisher expressly disclaim any responsibility for any errors, omissions, or adverse effects arising from the use or application of the information contained herein.

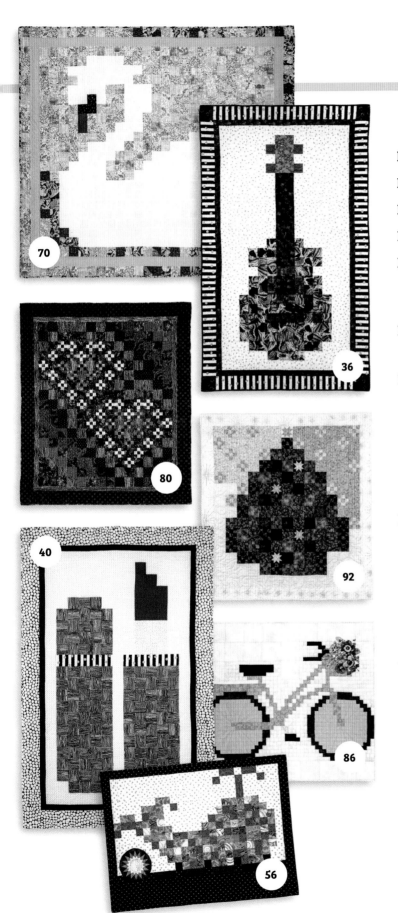

Contents

Introduction

Quilters have been cutting up larger pieces of fabric and cleverly stitching them back together to create all sorts of patterns for centuries. And it seems like each generation of quilters latches onto a style that's a little bit unique to the times. Not surprisingly in the age of technology, the pixelated bitmap approach (which I call "picture patchwork") is one that 21st century quilters have welcomed enthusiastically. By cutting and strategically joining hundreds of little squares of fabrics together, quilters can create charming images. My first design using this picture patchwork technique was such a rewarding and therapeutic process that I started looking for more inspiration. I quickly realized that cross-stitch graphs are also made with row after row of uniform squares. Luckily, many cross-stitch graphs are available for free download, and the artists are usually excited to see their designs interpreted in new ways!

In this book, I walk you through my picture patchwork process. I start with fabrics, the most important part of quilting, explaining a bit about how to choose fabrics, caring for your fabrics, and making color choices. Then, I explore some of the tools and materials that can make this journey much more enjoyable before explaining how to develop designs from cross-stitch graphs. Once you understand these basics, I describe the step-by-step picture patchwork process (including some helpful tips and tricks) and provide a brief guide for finishing your projects. Finally, the book includes 15 delightful projects, grouped into three sections based on difficulty. Start small with beginner quilts made from simple squares and build your skills up through advanced designs as you work on creating larger and more detailed images, mixing fabric piece sizes, and adding pre-pieced quilt blocks into your projects.

Each project includes written instructions and charts, so once you've organized your fabrics on your design board or wall to match the graph, "developing" your picture is just a matter of consistent sewing, careful pressing, and joining your rows together.

Whether you're looking to make a themed bed quilt, would like to add a unique wall hanging to your foyer, or want to create fun pieces to liven up your seasonal decorations, this book will take you there. Let's get started!

Jo Ann

Skyline Evergreen on page 92 combines the picture patchwork process with traditional Nine Patch blocks.

LESSON ONE:
Fabrics

I was raised in a home full of fabric and sewing was an everyday activity. My uncle owned a fabric importing business from the 1960s through the mid '70s. He was highly successful, and it was from him that I first learned a lot of what I know about fabric. My grandmother, mother, and aunt also all sewed to some extent, but none of them ever made a quilt. In their world, fabric was mainly for clothing and small home decor items. When I found quilting, it felt like I rediscovered fabric. Your fabric choices can make or break your finished piece.

Use high-quality fabrics. I cannot stress enough the value of using good-quality fabric for your quilts. I almost always quilt with 100 percent cotton fabrics and the only exception is the occasional silk, pulled from a stash I have left over from my former business. Quilting is a passion for most of us and we want the best results. Using the best materials will yield these results.

Think carefully about how your quilt will be used. Will the quilt be used every day and washed often? Are you making it for a child? Is it going to hang on a wall or be entered for competition? Quilts made for everyday use or for children will need to be made with more durable fabrics that should hold up to regular machine washing. Decorative and competition quilts require a bit more attention to detail. Crisp fabrics that can help create sharp points and details can make the process go smoothly.

High-quality 100 percent cotton fabrics are the best choice for picture patchwork (and quilting in general). This type of fabric is available in the variety of textures, colors, and shades needed to create a cohesive image.

These fabrics with darker, more saturated colors pop in your projects when you want to make a bold statement or find a strong contrast against a lighter background.

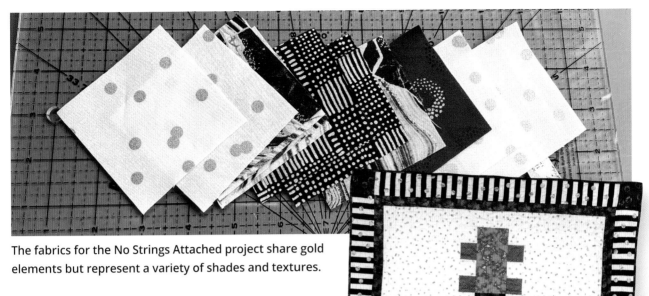

The fabrics for the No Strings Attached project share gold elements but represent a variety of shades and textures.

Consider color and value. For picture patchwork, the backgrounds need to contrast against the main image (dark on light or light on dark). The remaining design requires varying patterns and degrees of color intensity depending on what you are depicting. This color shading adds depth and perspective. The No Strings Attached project on page 36, for example, calls for a different fabric for every piece of the guitar. The fabrics coordinate and are within a similar color scheme, but

These fabrics all work well together because they share color and design elements. The patterns are also subtle enough that they could all work as neutrals or background fabrics, depending on the needs of the main image you're trying to create.

The finished No Strings Attached creates a recognizable and striking picture of a guitar by making sure each element has a distinct pattern.

the intensity and shade differences create definition between the parts. The light background contrasts against the dark main image, and the whole thing is pulled together with touches of gold and some pops of brilliant red.

Think about mixing prints and scale. Scale makes many contributions to a design. A large-scale print might not seem like the perfect choice for picture

I often gravitate toward strong floral prints in my pieces. Florals remind me of my childhood (my family had a florist's shop), and they are an easy way to create different shades in your pictures.

patchwork, but when you cut these larger designs up into smaller pieces, it often creates something quite different. Polka dots, stripes, and checks are often fantastic for creating contrasting textures and shades within an image and stripes are especially nice for creating borders and distinct bindings.

Don't forget about precuts. I usually prefer to cut my picture patchwork pieces from yardage, but precut squares and rolls are a convenient option if you don't want to do quite so much cutting.

Even having these suggestions as a guide, I have to admit that there are still times when my fabric planning is a bit more "fly by the seat of my pants." I go to my stash, cut some pieces from three or four fabrics I *think* will work, and puzzle the whole thing out on my design wall. Picking fabrics might seem a bit intimidating at first, but if you're working from a cross-stitch graph, it will likely include color suggestions. You just need to select quality fabrics that match the different shades on the graph.

Striped fabric is an easy choice for creating a striking border for almost any quilt.

If you're not in the mood to cut hundreds of small squares, fabric precuts are a great starting point for picture patchwork projects, particularly when they call for 2½" (6.4cm) squares.

LESSON TWO:
Other Supplies

While the right fabric makes your final designs sparkle, the right tools and supplies will help you refine your finished quilts and improve your skills. You may have some of these items in your sewing kit already, but how you use them can make a difference when creating picture patchwork pieces.

Cutting Mat—I use the ungridded side of my cutting mat. Most mats easily become worn in the same areas over and over because we tend to cut the same fabric sizes over and over (especially for these types of quilts). Using the blank side of the mat forces you to move around on the mat so you can avoid creating ridges in the surface.

Rotary Cutter—I prefer a straight-handled rotary cutter that includes a space for resting your thumb. If you prefer a cutter with a more ergonomic handle, use that style. Always be sure to cut away from yourself and

switch to a fresh blade often. For picture patchwork quilts, where you're cutting many small squares, you may even want to swap in a new blade halfway through cutting. When using cutters, people tend to drag their arm to push through a cut. Lift your arm at the elbow and put a bit of pressure on the blade. Your cuts will be much easier and will align better with your ruler.

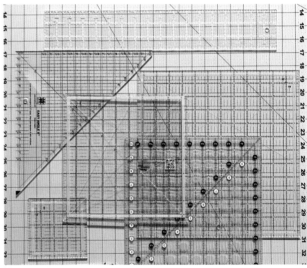

Rulers—Clear rulers come in many different shapes and sizes these days, and most have a multitude of uses. I tend to stick to the basics, but do prefer non-slip rulers. You can buy stick-on dots to add to rulers that weren't manufactured with the non-slip feature. Some people prefer specialty rulers (like Creative Grids Stripology rulers) that have cutting channels and are designed for cutting uniform strips and squares. These channels can cause burrs on rotary cutter blades. Cut carefully when using them. The key is to find a ruler you're comfortable using, as the picture patchwork process involves a lot of cutting (although you can work pre-cuts into your design).

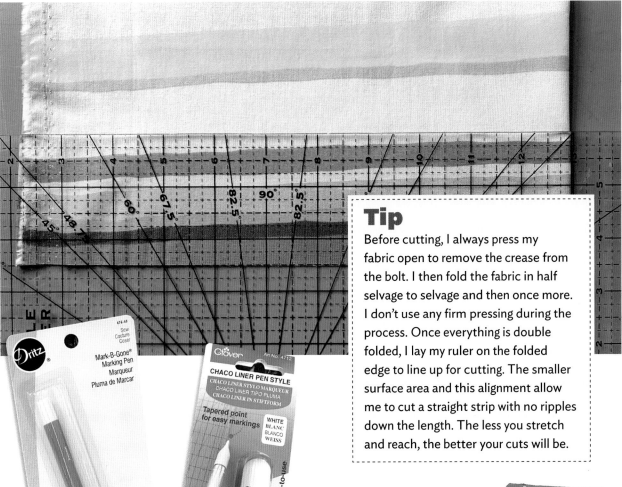

Tip

Before cutting, I always press my fabric open to remove the crease from the bolt. I then fold the fabric in half selvage to selvage and then once more. I don't use any firm pressing during the process. Once everything is double folded, I lay my ruler on the folded edge to line up for cutting. The smaller surface area and this alignment allow me to cut a straight strip with no ripples down the length. The less you stretch and reach, the better your cuts will be.

Marking Tools—Use water-soluble or chalk markers to label your squares with row numbers and directions to make sure you join them in the right order—a critical element in making picture patchwork quilts. There are dozens of options available. Make sure you use something that is removeable and have a light-colored one available for use on darker fabrics.

Straight Sewing Pins— Use quality pins to pin your fabric pieces together.

Quilt Clips—Once you've cut out your squares and planned your design, use quilt clips to keep each row of blocks organized and in order. I clip together the stacks of fabric squares until I'm ready to sew them together.

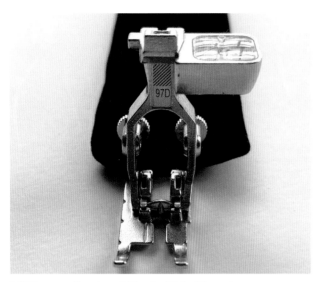

¼" Presser Foot and Single-Hole Throat Plate—I always use a ¼" presser foot and a single-hole throat plate. The presser foot ensures even seam lengths, while the throat plate supports the fabric to prevent distortion.

Thread—Stick with strong thread in neutral colors to match most fabrics. I prefer 100 percent cotton, but quilters do piece with blends as well. When you're putting hours of work in to create something beautiful, only good-quality thread will do.

Clip-On Light—I have a good light on my sewing machine, but I also use a clip-on mini light that I can bend into position to spotlight pieces I'm trying to focus on. Proper lighting is important to the process and also helps save your eyes from strain.

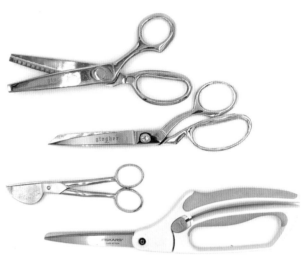

Scissors—Have a good, sharp pair of sewing scissors on hand, as well as a smaller detail scissors to clip threads.

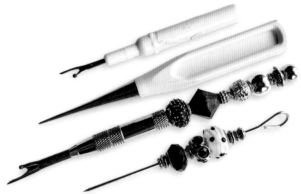

Stilettos and Seam Rippers—Stilettos are very useful when piecing, especially if the pieces are small. You can hold the pieces in place all the way through the sewing line using the small tip of the stiletto. Seam rippers are necessary, as well, for fixing any mistakes. The key is to keep a fresh one on hand, as they will dull after a bit of use.

This double-heart design (see page 80) was my first picture patchwork quilt, and inspired me to make more.

LESSON THREE:
Developing Designs

My patchwork picture designs come from many places, and often require a bit of time. I need to walk away and let things percolate before a truly solid idea develops. My best ideas tend to come to me in the middle of the night, so I keep a notebook on the nightstand next to my bed.

The quilts in this book are all a result of hours of surfing the internet, designing and fine-tuning with Electric Quilt 8 (EQ8—a robust computer program built for designing quilts), and scribbling on graph paper sheets. I have used Electric Quilt software for many years, upgrading each time a new version is available. It's very user-friendly and creates great results, particularly for adapting picture patchwork designs from cross-stitch graphs.

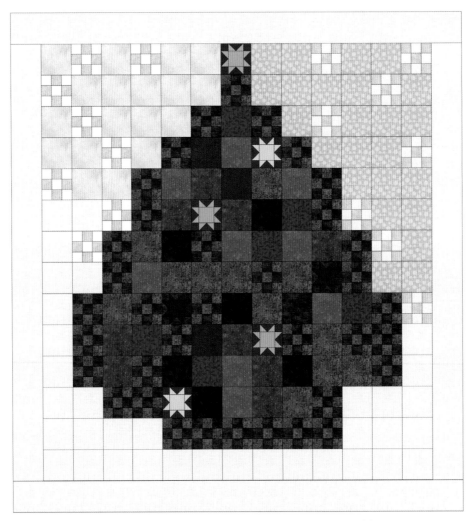

EQ8 has the added advantage of testing out the look of common fabric patterns and textures within the program.

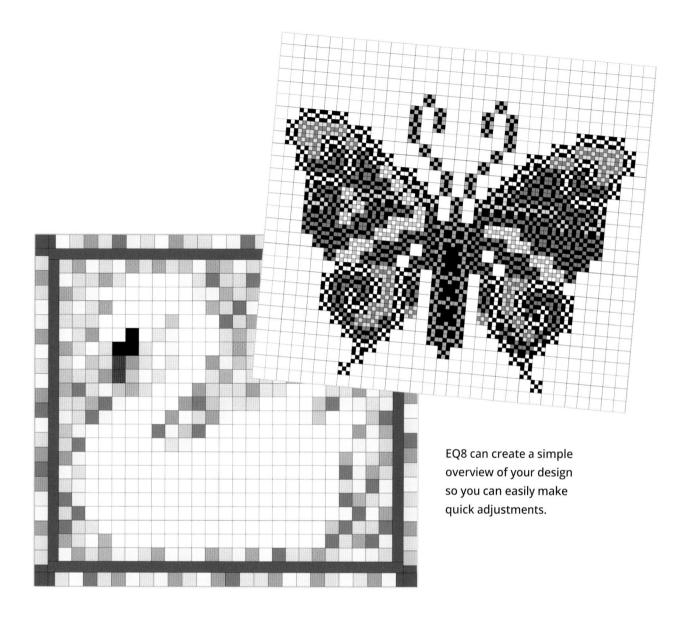

EQ8 can create a simple overview of your design so you can easily make quick adjustments.

For me, the most fun part of the design process is looking at cross-stitch charts and woven bracelet graphs and determining whether they would work with fabric squares. Since cross-stitch patterns and bracelet graphs are made on a grid, many lend themselves to picture patchwork. It's not always a one-to-one translation, however—a small section of flowers might need to be revised to keep it from getting overly complicated, for example. The biggest issue is that the designs explode in size. Cross-stitch, needlepoint, and other types of embroidery are normally created on a very small scale,

and the same is true for bracelet weaving. Moving the design up to 1" (2.5cm) or larger squares creates a much bigger finished piece.

One of the first things I do is convert my design inspiration to black and white. This is helpful in determining the values of the piece and the scales required for creating different colored sections. I then look for areas that can be combined into larger fabric pieces or created with other sewing techniques (for example, I'll often add flowers using larger sections of floral fabric or via appliqué after the piecing is finished).

Step-by-Step: From Inspiration to Quilt Top

A simple example of how to turn a cross-stitch graph into a quilt top is this train design from Susan Penny, editor of UK-based *CrossStitcher* magazine. The original design for cross-stitching is smaller than 2" (5.1cm) square and intended to be used as a mini design or motif. For patchwork purposes, each cross-stitch becomes a fabric square (in this case, I used 2½" [6.4cm] squares and some 2½" [6.4cm] half-square triangles). The resulting quilt top measures 34½" x 28½" (87.3 x 72.4cm) when the borders are cut 2½" (6.4cm) wide.

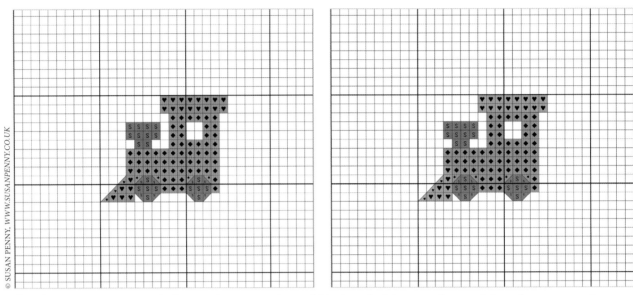

© SUSAN PENNY, WWW.SUSANPENNY.CO.UK

1. Choose your cross-stitch design. View it in color and black and white to understand the values you need to replicate in fabric.

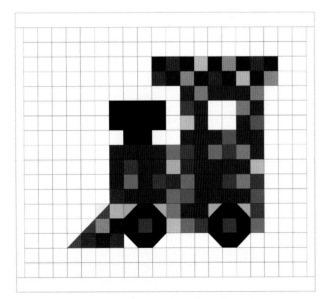

2. Create your own design chart based on the chosen image. If you use a program like EQ, it will automatically tell you what the finished quilt top size will be.

3. Select your fabric and follow the steps in Lesson Four, beginning on page 18, to finish your quilt top.

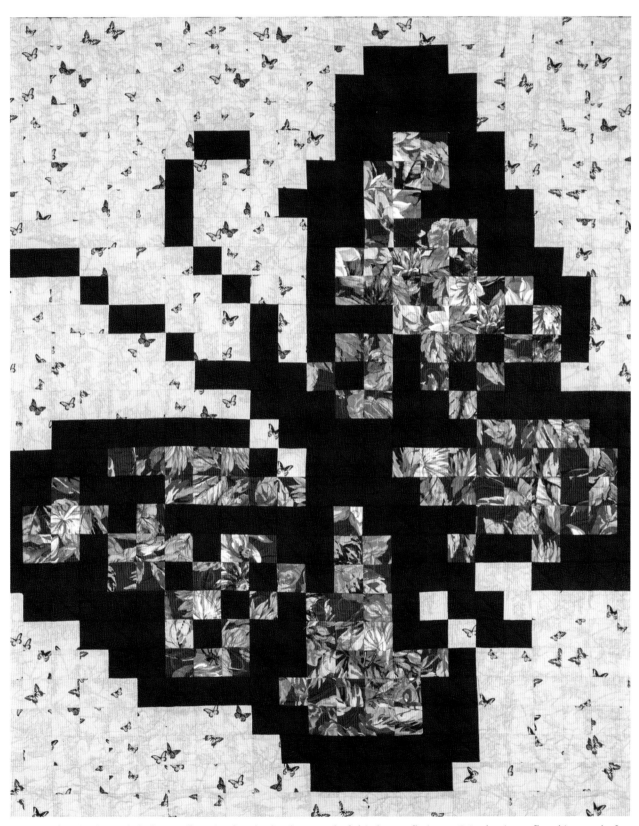

How perfect is this subtle butterfly print for the background of this butterfly image? And using a floral instead of an orange solid adds so much more interest.

How to Make a Picture Patchwork Quilt Top

Each of the quilts in this book follows this basic set of instructions. The keys to success are consistent cutting, using a design wall or board to keep track of your fabric squares, maintaining a consistent ¼" (6.4mm) seam allowance, proper pressing, and following the color-coded Quilt Diagram provided for each pattern. I've also provided a matching color-coded Detail Breakdown of the first few rows of each design to get you started.

Following the Diagrams

Fabric Colors

Fabric A: White & Dots

Fabric B: Assorted Blues

Fabric C: Navy Blue & Dots

Fabric D: Midnight Blue & Dots

Each project includes Fabric Requirements and Cutting Instructions charts and a color-coded key that shows you how those charts relate to the Detail Breakdown and Quilt Diagram.

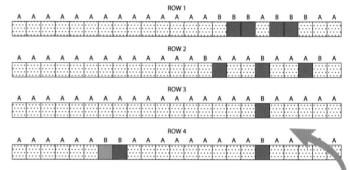

The color-coded Detail Breakdown shows how the first few rows are constructed. Each row and color is labeled.

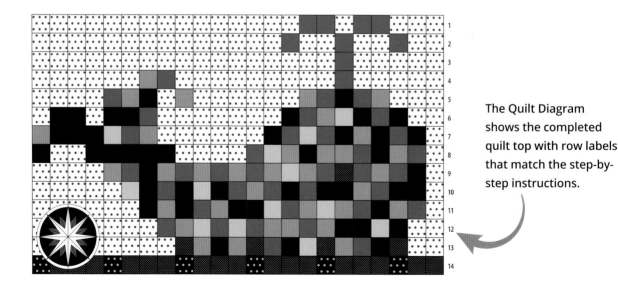

The Quilt Diagram shows the completed quilt top with row labels that match the step-by-step instructions.

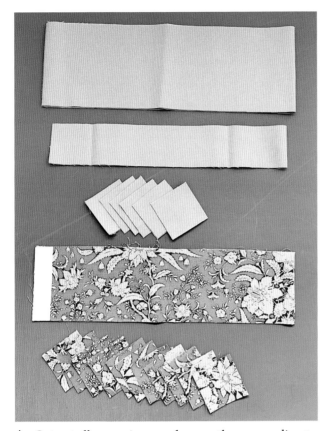

1. Cut out all your pieces and group them according to the color code for your pattern.

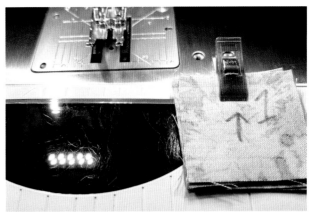

3. Once you are happy with your layout, pick up the individual squares from left to right, working in horizontal rows. Place each square on top of the previous one (the one to the left) and create a neat stack. Turn the last fabric square of each row wrong side up, then use a water-soluble or chalk marker to label the square with the row number. Clip or pin each stacked row together.

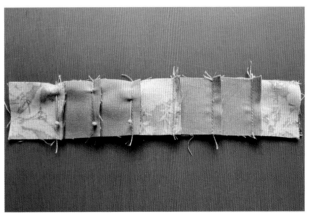

4. Stitch the squares in each row together using a stitch length appropriate for piecing quilt blocks. On most machines, I use a stitch length of 2–2.5.

2. Starting with Row 1 of the grid, place the corresponding units on your design wall or board. Continue working across each row, consulting the color-coded quilt diagram and counting across the rows as needed. Lay out the entire quilt.

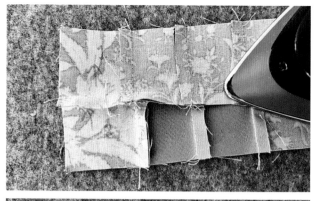

5. Press each row carefully, with the seams in opposite directions so you can butt the seams together when connecting the horizontal rows.

7. Press the combined rows carefully to finish your quilt top. I recommend pressing all the rows toward the bottom of the quilt.

8. Square your quilt top and add borders according to the individual quilt design instructions, then press the borders outward, away from the quilt center.

9. Layer, quilt, and bind as desired (refer to Binding on page 23).

6. Align the bottom of Row 1 to the top of Row 2, pin them together so your seams properly line up in opposite directions, then sew them together. Repeat with the remaining rows, joining them in numerical order from top to bottom.

Construction Tips & Tricks

Poor workmanship is my pet peeve! Anyone who has taken classes with me knows this all too well. Because of this, I've come up with a few tips and tricks over the years to keep the quilting process organized and remove any potential stressors. My methods help me create precise quilts with stellar finishing every time.

- My number-one tip is to *press*—don't iron back and forth. Be sure to carefully press your fabrics and projects every step of the way. I use prefer using steam during this process.

- I am a pressing fanatic. I press all my fabrics at the start of each project and fold them neatly over hangers. The creases and folds in fabric yardage are, to me, little monsters that can sneak into your project and create unnecessary stress.

- Most fabric is wrapped onto a cardboard bolt mechanically, creating an unsightly crease down the center. Press this stubborn crease away with a liquid pressing agent or one part liquid starch diluted with two parts of water.

- Don't "torture" your fabric by stretching or forcing it. Handle it gently.

- Don't be afraid to mark the wrong sides of your blocks. I use a water-soluble marker, pencil, or even plain old sidewalk chalk. With that being said—be aware of what color fabric you are marking so that it does not show through and be sure that marks can be removed if needed. For the quilts in this book, I did a lot of labeling with numbers and directional arrows to keep my rows in order.

- I use a design wall or a design board religiously. Mine is made from a sheet of foam core insulation board that is covered with a layer of batting and then a layer of gridded flannel. My board measures 4' x 7' (1.2 x 2.1m) but is still light and easy to maneuver (even in my small sewing studio). This type of space is a necessity, particularly for quilt projects like these.

- Be kind to your tools and keep them in good working order. Change your rotary blade when it needs to be changed and change the needle on your sewing machine often.

- Use high-quality pins when joining fabrics together or arranging them on your design surface.

- I use a stiletto when piecing at my sewing machine to hold pieces in place and keep my seams even right up through the end of the stitching line.

LESSON FIVE:
Finishing

Finishing is often not given the attention it deserves, but it is the final piece that creates an elevated picture patchwork quilt. Keep the following items in mind to achieve a perfect finish every time.

- **Square your top by measuring all four sides of the quilt top.** Each side should be equal if square, or, if rectangular, the parallel sides should equal each other. If the measurements don't match, trim carefully to the correct finished dimensions.

- **Choose appropriate batting and backing fabric for your quilt.** The right backing and batting will make the difference between you just liking your quilt and truly loving your quilt. Choose a color and pattern for your backing fabric that will enhance your quilt design or simply blend so as not to overwhelm the quilt front. The batting should provide the right amount of stability and thickness.

- **Make and commit to a method of quilting.** Whether it's hand quilting, machine quilting, midarm, longarm, or tying—decide on one and plan accordingly. Carefully choose your quilting thread colors. High contrast quilts present the greatest challenge—do you go with a dark thread, a light thread, or something in between? Beige, soft green, gray, or subtly variegated threads often work well on both light and dark fabrics.

- **Prepare the binding and attach it to the quilt.** I use a traditional binding technique with 2½" (6.4cm) wide strips. Follow the detailed binding instructions on pages 23–25.

- **Add a label to the back of the quilt.** These labels are your final chance to personalize your piece. It's your signature as the artist.

Your quilt label should clearly indicate the name of the quilt. I also include my information and the date.

Binding

Once your quilt is quilted, whether you do it or take it to a quilting service, and you have trimmed away the excess batting and backing, the final step is to bind your quilt. This creates a finished edge around your quilt. Binding strips are cut from the width of fabric (WOF), which is generally 44" (1.1m) wide. For example, if you need 175" (4.4m) of binding, you will cut four strips (175" [4.4m] divided by 44" [1.1m] equals 3.97 strips) and join them together. Keep in mind that when you join your recommended 2¼" (5.7cm) wide strips with the method shown, you will lose approximately 3" (7.6cm) in length with each join, so make sure to cut enough strips; too long is always better than too short.

Calculating Binding

To determine the binding length for your quilt, these are the calculations you'll need:

- Measure your quilt length and width, multiply by 2, add together, and add 10" (25.4cm).

- Since standard quilting cotton is 42"–45" (1.07–1.14m) wide, estimate your useable fabric width (minus the selvages) at 40" (1m).

- The most common binding strips are 2¼"–2½" (5.7–6.4cm) wide.

For example:

- Assuming your quilt is 36" x 60" (91cm x 1.5m), double 36" to 72" (1.8m) and 60" to 120" (3.1m). Add together: 72 + 120 = 192. Add 10 for a total of 202" (5.1m) of binding.

- Divide 202" (5.1m) by 40" (1m) to determine the number of strips needed. In this case, it's 5.05 (or 5.1) strips. Always round up, so you'll want to cut 6 strips.

- Multiply the number of strips (6) by the width of your strips (2½" [6.4cm]). This will yield how much fabric you need: 15" (38.4cm) of 40" (1m) wide fabric.

Binding can be a solid color, scrappy joined fabrics, or a print. Experiment to figure out what looks best with each design.

Joining Binding Ends

To join binding strips smoothly and avoid a lump along the edge of your quilt or project, it is best to join the strips with an angled seam rather than just placing right sides together and stitching a straight seam from edge to edge.

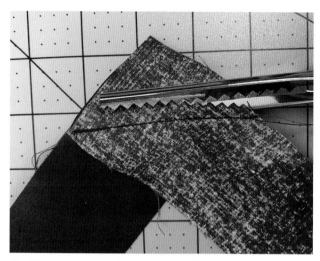

2. Trim the seam allowance to ¼" (6.4mm) with pinking shears.

 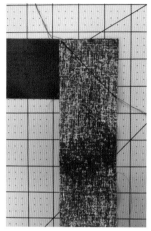

1. Join binding strips by overlapping the end of one strip perpendicular and right sides together with the end of a second strip. You should have a backward L shape. Draw a diagonal line from the upper outer corner of your top strip to the lower inner corner of your bottom strip. Pin if desired. Stitch a diagonal seam directly on top of your guideline.

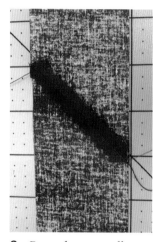 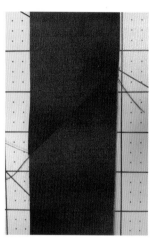

3. Press the seam allowance open.

Binding Quilt Edges

I recommend double-fold binding: cutting the strips, joining them, then pressing them in half lengthwise. If you attach your binding to the front of your quilt, I recommend folding over to the back and whipstitching by hand to secure to the backing. If you prefer to machine finish, stitch the binding first to the back side of your quilt, fold to the front, and machine edge stitch to secure.

Binding with a Whipstitch Finish

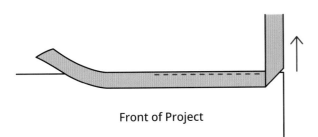

Front of Project

1. Fold the binding strip in half lengthwise, wrong sides together. With raw edges aligned, start stitching your binding to the quilt edge, beginning on one side and leaving at least 5" (12.7cm) of unstitched binding as a tail. As you approach the corner, stop stitching ¼" (6.4mm) before you reach the edge. Fix (or lock) your stitching. Fold the binding up at a 90-degree angle.

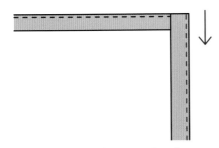

2. Fold the binding back down so that the raw edge of the binding is flush with the raw edge of the quilt and the top fold is aligned with the original side. Begin stitching where you left off on the previous side, making sure to fix your stitch line at the starting point. Continue around the quilt, stopping approximately 7"–8" (17.8–20.3cm) from your starting point.

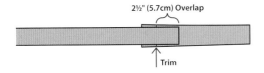

2½" (5.7cm) Overlap

Trim

3. Place the tails smooth and flat along the quilt edge. The overlap will need to be the same amount as the width of your binding. For a 2¼" (5.7cm) binding, overlay 2¼" (5.7cm). Clip the excess ends of the tails perpendicular to the edge of the quilt.

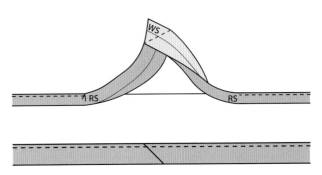

WS

RS   RS

4. Place the ends right sides together at right angles. Stitch a diagonal line from corner to corner and trim off the corner, leaving a ¼" (6.4mm) seam allowance (top diagram). Now simply finger-press the binding into its original folded shape along the remaining raw edge of the quilt. Press, pin, and continue stitching to secure, fixing your stitch line as you start and stop (bottom diagram).

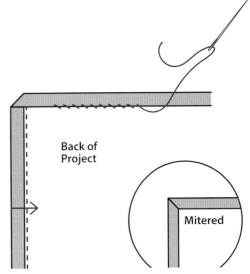

Back of Project

Mitered

5. Press the binding away from the front edge and fold it over to the back of the quilt. Miter the binding at the corner and hand whipstitch into place with a single thread.

Beginner Quilt Projects

The quilts in this section are beginner projects, constructed from simple square or rectangular blocks in one or two sizes that are used repeatedly. The color guides are included, but substitutions are always allowed. A simple grid layout illustration is provided to help you assemble the design. I recommend using a design wall or board to lay out each of the background and design blocks as shown on the quilt diagram. Each quilt is completed by sewing the blocks into horizontal rows and then sewing those rows together in order. I've also added simple straight borders to frame some of the projects.

Garden Buffet

There are plenty of sweet flowers for this bee to feast on! This colorful quilt is easy enough for you to make in an afternoon and is perfect to display in a sunny spot. It's made up of small rectangular blocks that are just as easy to stitch as squares.

Finished quilt measurements: 27" x 32" (68.6 x 81.3cm)

Fabric Requirements

Fabric A	8–10 fat quarters	assorted floral prints
Fabric B	8–10 fat quarters	assorted green prints
Fabric C	1 fat quarter	black tonal print
Fabric D	1 fat quarter	yellow tonal print
Fabric E	1 fat quarter	gray tonal print
Fabric F	¼ yd. (22.9cm)	gold tonal print
Fabric G	¾ yd. (68.6cm)	black tonal print

Cutting Instructions

Fabric A	102 rectangles	1½" x 2½" (3.8 x 6.4cm)
Fabric B	68 rectangles	1½" x 2½" (3.8 x 6.4cm)
Fabric C	24 rectangles	1½" x 2½" (3.8 x 6.4cm)
Fabric D	14 rectangles	1½" x 2½" (3.8 x 6.4cm)
Fabric E	20 rectangles	1½" x 2½" (3.8 x 6.4cm)
Fabric F	4 strips	1½" (3.8cm) x WOF
Fabric G	4 strips	3½" (8.9cm) x WOF

> **Precut-friendly design!**
> Use 2½" (6.4cm) strips.

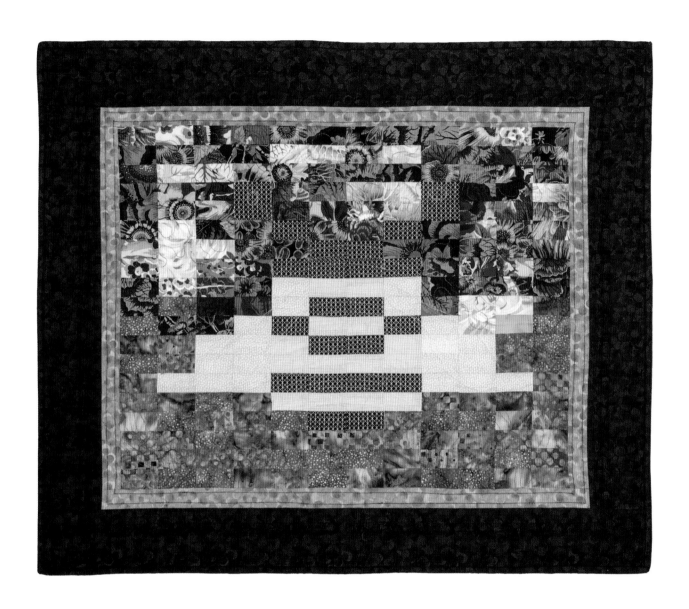

Fabric Colors

Fabric A:
Assorted Florals

Fabric B:
Assorted Greens

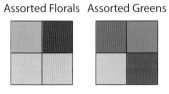

Fabric C:
Black Tonal

Fabric D:
Yellow Tonal

Fabric E:
Gray Tonal

Fabric F:
Gold Tonal

Fabric G:
Black Tonal Border

Quilt Construction

You will join 12 rectangles across 19 rows. Consult Lesson Four: How to Make a Picture Patchwork Quilt Top on page 18 as needed.

1. On your design board or wall, arrange your Fabric A rectangles into Rows 1 through 3.

2. Starting on Row 4, introduce Fabric C rectangles, consulting the quilt diagram for placement. Continue following the diagram.

3. Starting on Row 9, introduce Fabric D and Fabric E rectangles to begin forming the body and wings of the bee. Continue following the diagram.

4. Starting on Row 12, the background switches from Fabric A rectangles to Fabric B rectangles. Continue following the diagram until all the rectangles in this central section are placed.

5. Collect the rectangles in order from left to right. Turn over and label the wrong side of the last rectangle, and then clip them together until you're ready to sew.

6. Stitch the rectangles in each horizontal row together, then carefully press the seams of each row in opposite directions.

7. Join the horizontal rows in numerical order from top to bottom to form the quilt center.

8. Carefully press the quilt top. I recommend pressing all the row seams toward the bottom of the quilt.

9. Cut two of the Fabric F border strips to match the left and right edge measurements of the quilt. Add the Fabric F border strips to the left and right edges of the quilt. Repeat with the top and bottom edges.

10. Add the Fabric G border strips to the Fabric F border in the same way.

11. Press all the border seams away from the quilt center.

12. Finish your quilt as desired.

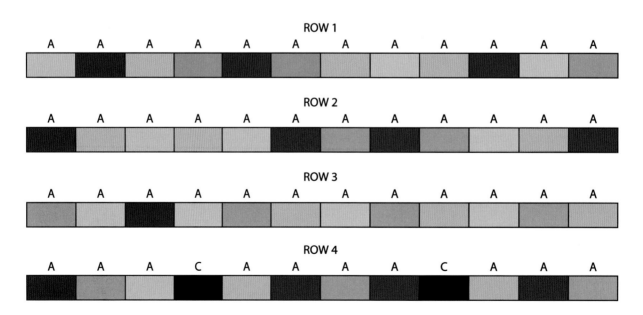

Detail: Rows 1–4

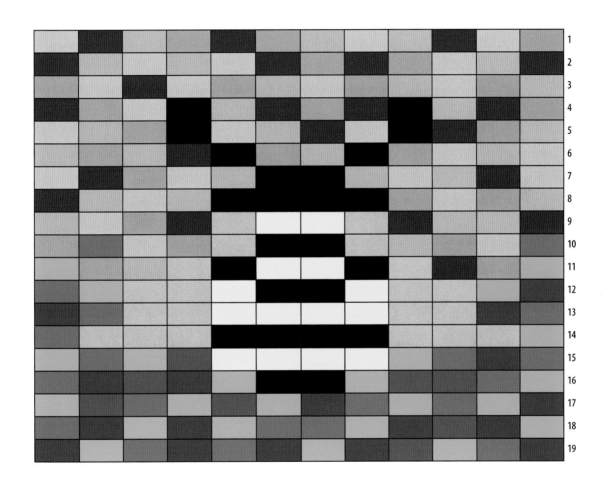

Quilt Diagram

Flutterby

Butterflies often visit the flower boxes along our deck. In my search for inspiration, I found this collection of fabric and ran with it—my own celebration of these beautiful visitors. Adjust the colors to remember your own meaningful encounters with nature.

Finished quilt measurements: 55" x 55" (1.4 x 1.4m)

Fabric Requirements

Fabric A	2 yds. (1.8m)	beige butterfly print
Fabric B	1 yd. (91.4cm)	black solid
Fabric C	⅝ yd. (57.2cm)	orange floral print

Cutting Instructions

Fabric A	435 squares	2½" (6.4cm)
Fabric B	222 squares	2½" (6.4cm)
Fabric C	127 squares	2½" (6.4cm)

Precut-friendly design!
Use 2½" (6.4cm) strips or square packs.

Fabric Colors

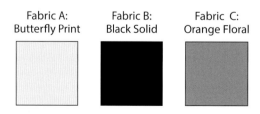

Fabric A: Butterfly Print   Fabric B: Black Solid   Fabric C: Orange Floral

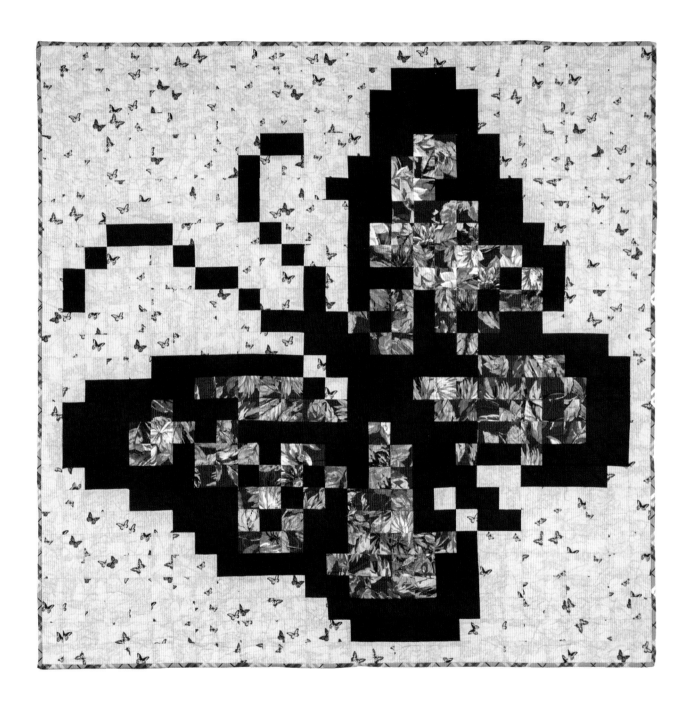

Quilt Construction

You will join 28 squares across 28 rows. Consult Lesson Four: How to Make a Picture Patchwork Quilt Top on page 18 as needed.

1. On your design board or wall, arrange your Fabric A squares into Row 1.

2. Starting on Row 2, introduce Fabric B squares, consulting the quilt diagram for placement. Continue following the diagram.

3. Starting on Row 5, introduce Fabric C squares, consulting the quilt diagram for placement. Continue following the diagram until all the squares are placed.

4. Collect the squares in order from left to right. Turn over and label the wrong side of the last square, and then clip them together until you're ready to sew.

5. Stitch the units in each horizontal row together, then carefully press the seams of each row in opposite directions.

6. Join the horizontal rows in numerical order from top to bottom to form the quilt center.

7. Carefully press the quilt top. I recommend pressing all the row seams toward the bottom of the quilt.

8. Finish your quilt as desired.

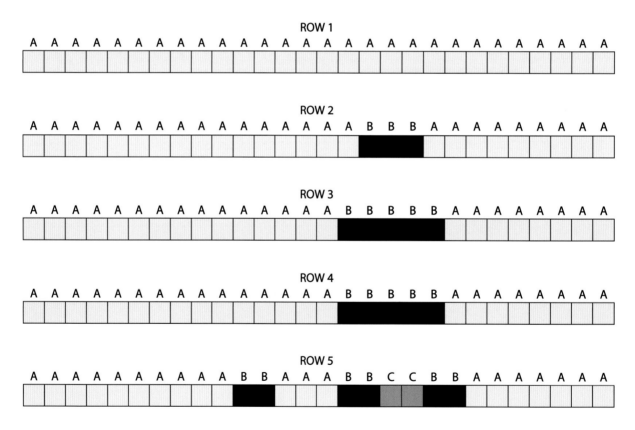

Detail Breakdown: Rows 1–5

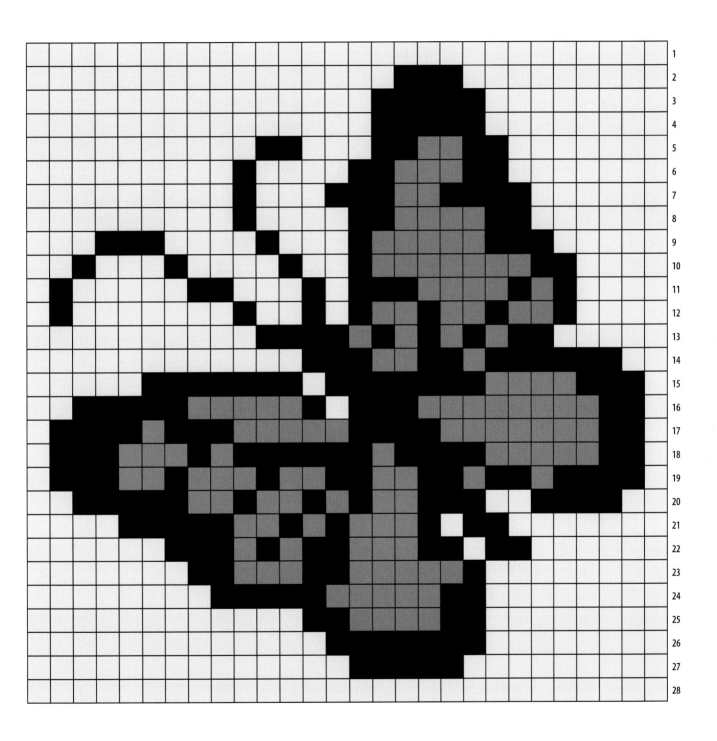

Quilt Diagram

No Strings Attached

This is a great project for those "wannabe" rock stars. Everyone knows someone who would love to strum a few strings and write a few songs—with this quilt, they can snuggle for a nap while dreaming of their own music.

Finished quilt measurements: 45" x 75" (1.1 x 1.9m)

Fabric Requirements

Fabric A	1½ yds. (1.4m)	white & gold dot print
Fabric B	½ yd. (45.7cm)	black & gold marble print
Fabric C	1 yd. (91.4cm)	black & gold circle print
Fabric D	1 fat quarter	light gray (black & silver) print
Fabric E	1 fat quarter	gray stone print
Fabric F	1 fat quarter	dark gray (black & silver) print
Fabric G	1 fat quarter	red circle print
Fabric H	1 yd. (91.4cm)	black & white stripe with gold dot print

Cutting Instructions

Fabric A	234 squares	3" (7.6cm)
Fabric B	80 squares	3" (7.6cm)
Fabric C	24 squares	3" (7.6cm)
	5 strips	2" (5.1cm) x WOF
Fabric D	8 squares	3" (7.6cm)
Fabric E	8 squares	3" (7.6cm)
Fabric F	4 squares	3" (7.6cm)
Fabric G	4 squares	4" (10.2cm)
	6 squares	3" (7.6cm)
Fabric H	5 strips	4" (10.2cm) x WOF

Fabric Colors

Fabric A:
White Gold
Dots

Fabric B:
Black & Gold
Marble

Fabric C:
Black & Gold
Circles

Fabric D:
Light Gray

Fabric E:
Gray Stone

Fabric F:
Dark Gray

Fabric G:
Red Circles

Fabric H:
Black & White
Stripes

Quilt Construction

You will join 14 squares across 26 rows.
Consult Lesson Four: How to Make a Picture Patchwork
Quilt Top on page 18 as needed.

1. On your design board or wall, arrange your Fabric A squares into Row 1.

2. Starting on Row 2, introduce Fabric E squares, consulting the quilt diagram for placement. Continue following the diagram.

3. Starting on Row 3, introduce Fabric F squares, consulting the quilt diagram for placement. Continue following the diagram.

4. Starting on Row 6, introduce Fabric C squares, consulting the quilt diagram for placement. Continue following the diagram.

5. Starting on Row 16, introduce Fabric D squares, consulting the quilt diagram for placement. Continue following the diagram.

6. Starting on Row 19, introduce the 3" (7.6cm) Fabric G squares, consulting the quilt diagram for placement. Continue following the diagram until all the squares in this central section are placed.

7. Collect the squares in order from left to right. Turn over and label the wrong side of the last square, and then clip them together until you're ready to sew.

8. Stitch the units in each horizontal row together, then carefully press the seams of each row in opposite directions.

9. Join the horizontal rows in numerical order from top to bottom to form the quilt center.

10. Carefully press the quilt top. I recommend pressing all the row seams toward the bottom of the quilt.

11. Cut two of the Fabric C border strips to match the left and right edge measurements of the quilt. Add the Fabric C border strips to the left and right edges of the quilt. Repeat with the top and bottom edges.

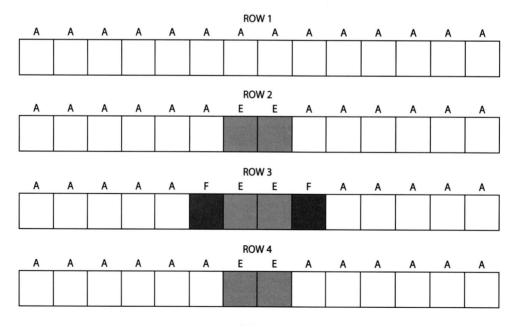

Detail: Rows 1–4

12. Cut two of the Fabric H border strips to match the top and bottom edge measurements of the quilt. Sew 4" (10.2cm) Fabric G squares to both ends of these strips. Add the Fabric H border strip units to the top and bottom edges of the Fabric C border.

13. Cut the remaining Fabric H border strips to match the left and right edge measurements of the quilt. Add the Fabric H border strips to the left and right edges of the Fabric C border.

14. Press all the border seams away from the quilt center.

15. Finish your quilt as desired.

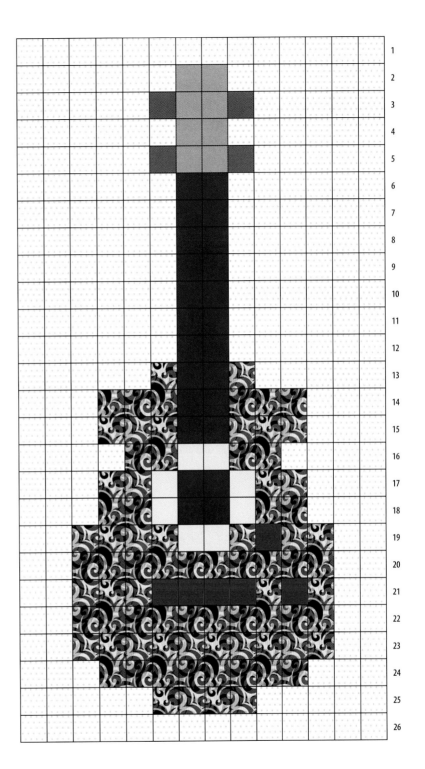

Quilt Diagram

My Favorite Shade

Choosing lipsticks is always a challenge for me—I always seem to end up buying the same color. Make this quilt in your favorite shade or try something completely different! You can even change up the case colors and embellish the finished design with anything from decorative stitches to rhinestones. This is the perfect design for a glamour girl!

Finished quilt measures: 51" x 78" (1.3 x 2m)

Fabric Requirements

Fabric A	1½ yds. (1.4m)	white & black dot print
Fabric B	1¼ yds. (1.1m)	black & white stripe print
Fabric C	fat quarter	magenta print
Fabric D	fat quarter	white & gold dot print
Fabric E	fat quarter	black, white & gold print
Fabric F	½ yd. (45.7cm)	black solid
Fabric G	1½ yds. (1.4m)	black dot print

Cutting Instructions

Fabric A	60 squares	3" (7.6cm)
	6 strips	3½" (8.9cm) x WOF
Fabric B	129 squares	3" (7.6cm)
Fabric C	12 squares	3" (7.6cm)
Fabric D	9 squares	3" (7.6cm)
Fabric E	2 rectangles	3" x 15" (7.6 x 38.1cm)
Fabric F	6 strips	2" (5.1cm) x WOF
Fabric G	7 strips	5" (12.7cm) x WOF

Fabric Colors

Fabric A: White & Black Dots

Fabric B: Black & White Stripes

Fabric C: Magenta

Fabric D: White & Gold

Fabric E: Black, White, & Gold Stripes

Fabric F: Black (1st Border)

Fabric G: Black with Dots (2nd Border)

Quilt Construction

You will join 11 squares across 20 rows.
Consult Lesson Four: How to Make a Picture Patchwork
Quilt Top on page 18 as needed.

1. On your design board or wall, arrange your Fabric A and Fabric C squares into Rows 1 through 4, consulting the quilt diagram for placement.

2. Starting on Row 4, introduce Fabric B squares, alternating horizontal and vertical stripe alignment and consulting the quilt diagram for placement. Continue following the diagram.

3. Starting on Row 7, introduce Fabric D squares, consulting the quilt diagram for placement. Continue following the diagram.

4. On Row 10, introduce the Fabric E rectangles, consulting the quilt diagram for placement. Continue following the diagram until all the fabric pieces in this central section are placed.

5. Collect the squares in order from left to right. Turn over and label the wrong side of the last square, and then clip them together until you're ready to sew.

6. Stitch the units in each horizontal row together, then carefully press the seams of each row in opposite directions.

7. Join the horizontal rows in numerical order from top to bottom to form the quilt center.

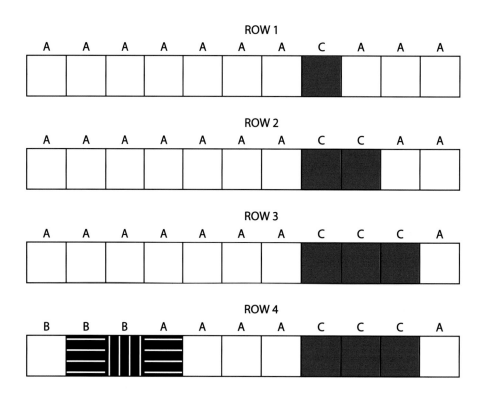

Detail: Rows 1–4

8. Carefully press the quilt top. I recommend pressing all the row seams toward the bottom of the quilt.

9. Join the Fabric A border strips together, then cut this larger strip to match the right and left edge measurements of the quilt. Add the Fabric A border strips to the left and right edges of the quilt. Repeat to add Fabric A border strips to the top and bottom edges.

10. Add the Fabric F border strips to the Fabric A border in the same way.

11. Add the Fabric G border strips to the Fabric F border in the same way.

12. Press all the border seams away from the quilt center.

13. Finish your quilt as desired.

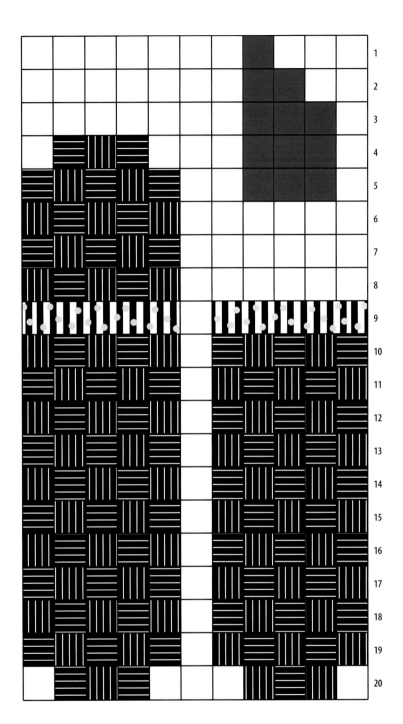

Quilt Diagram

Jimmie Shoo

Shoes are perhaps the most important accessory in the world of fashion! Just like quilts, they're created in every color of the rainbow and each tiny embellishment tells a story. Even the soles are designed to make a statement. Adjust the colors and fabrics used in this design to make your own statement.

Finished quilt measurements: 49" x 38" (1.2m x 96.5cm)

Fabric Requirements

Fabric A	1 yd. (91.4cm)	beige solid
Fabric B	⅝ yd. (57.2cm)	black and purple print
Fabric C	¾ yd. (68.6cm)	dark gray pebbles print
Fabric D	¼ yd. (22.9cm)	lilac solid
Fabric E	½ yd. (45.7cm)	black floral print
Fabric F	⅞ yd. (80cm)	gray and white circle print

Cutting Instructions

Fabric A	223 squares	2" (5.1cm)
Fabric B	124 squares	2" (5.1cm)
Fabric C	35 squares	2" (5.1cm)
	5 strips	2½" (6.4cm) x WOF
Fabric D	25 squares	2" (5.1cm)
Fabric E	87 squares	2" (5.1cm)
Fabric F	6 strips	3½" (8.9cm) x WOF

Fabric Colors

Fabric A: Beige Solid	Fabric B: Black & Purple	Fabric C: Dark Gray Pebbles	Fabric D: Lilac Solid	Fabric E: Black Floral	Fabric F: Gray & White Circles

Quilt Construction

You will join 26 squares across 19 rows.
Consult Lesson Four: How to Make a Picture Patchwork Quilt Top on page 18 as needed.

1. On your design board or wall, arrange your Fabric A squares into Row 1.

2. Starting on Row 2, introduce Fabric B squares, consulting the quilt diagram for placement. Continue following the diagram.

3. Starting on Row 7, introduce Fabric E squares, consulting the quilt diagram for placement. Continue following the diagram.

4. Starting on Row 8, introduce Fabric C squares, consulting the quilt diagram for placement. Continue following the diagram.

5. Starting on Row 10, introduce Fabric D squares, consulting the quilt diagram for placement. Continue following the diagram until all the squares in this central section are placed.

6. Collect the squares in order from left to right. Turn over and label the wrong side of the last square, and then clip them together until you're ready to sew.

7. Stitch the units in each horizontal row together, then carefully press the seams of each row in opposite directions.

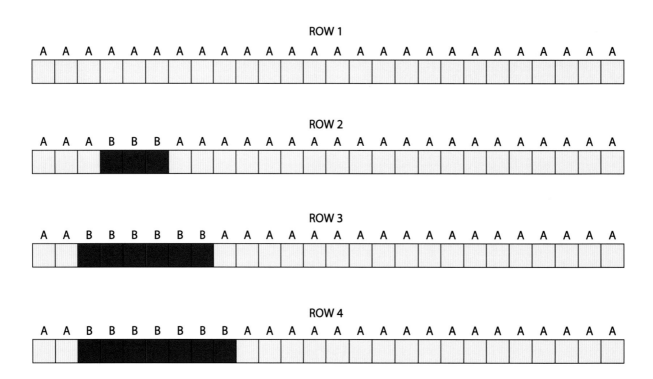

Detail: Rows 1–4

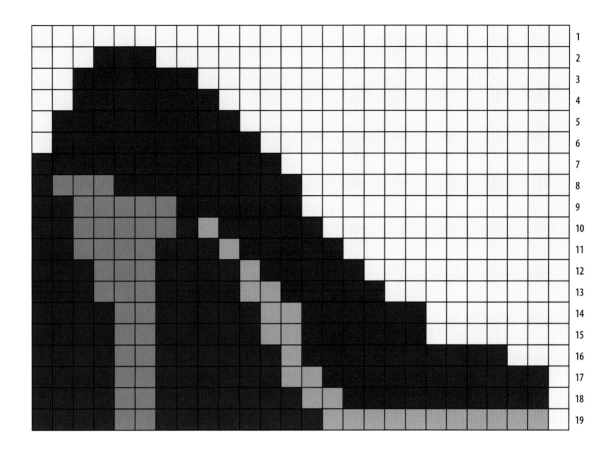

Quilt Diagram

8. Join the horizontal rows in numerical order from top to bottom to form the quilt center.

9. Carefully press the quilt top. I recommend pressing all the row seams toward the bottom of the quilt.

10. Join the Fabric C border strips together, then cut this larger strip to match the right and left edge measurements of the quilt. Add the Fabric C border strips to the left and right edges of the quilt. Repeat to add Fabric C border strips to the top and bottom edges.

11. Add the Fabric F border strips to the Fabric C border in the same way.

12. Press all the border seams away from the quilt center.

13. Finish your quilt as desired.

Intermediate Quilt Projects

These projects are a bit more of a challenge. Some are created in sections or as units of rows that are later joined together. They feature different fabric sizes and strips to add interest and fill in the backgrounds more quickly. They also feature more complex patterns and the option to add unique pieced blocks or customized designs. It's time to think a little bit before you cut!

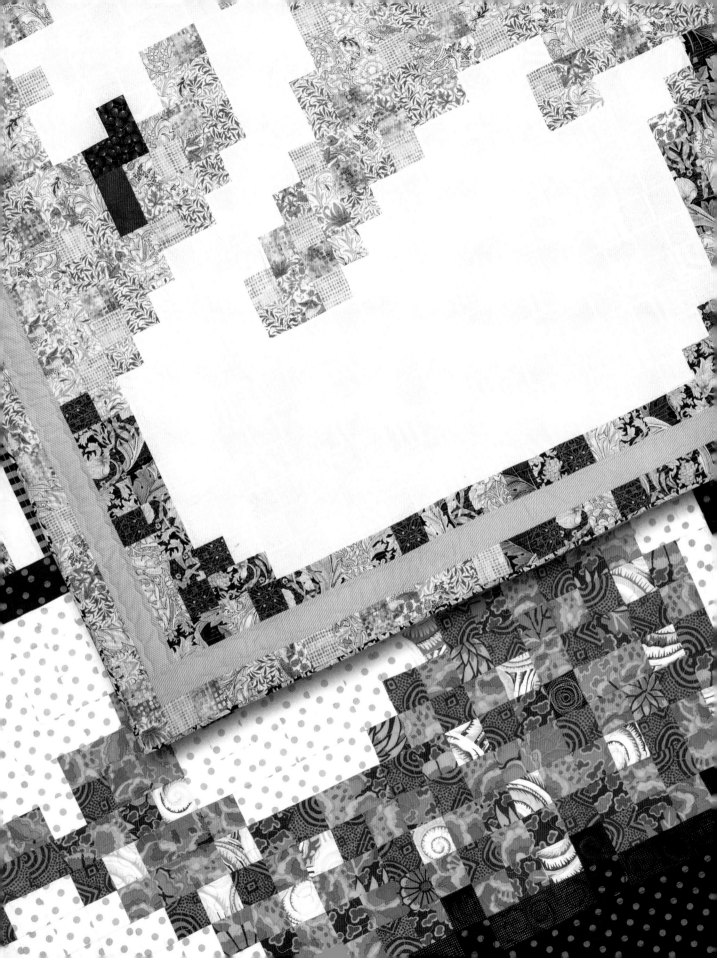

Perfect Layers

I wish I could bake a fancy layered cake just like this one. Since it's unlikely I'll ever achieve that goal, I've created my own fabric version. This piece uses some different methods to create the final effect—building the cake layer by layer rather than row by row. I spent hours sifting through various designs and adjusting my own process to create just the right recipe!

Finished quilt measures: 36" x 36" (91.4 x 91.4cm)

Fabric Requirements

Fabric A	1½ yds. (1.4m)	white on white print
Fabric B	½ yd. (45.7cm)	white dot print
Fabric C	fat quarter	gray dot print
Fabric D	fat quarter	pink dot print
Fabric E	fat quarter	seafoam dot print
Fabric F	fat eighth	white & silver print

Cutting Instructions

Fabric A	2 rectangles	6½" x 36" (16.5 x 91.4cm)
	2 rectangles	6½" x 12½" (16.5 x 31.8cm)
	2 rectangles	5" x 11½" (12.7 x 29.2cm)
	2 rectangles	6" x 8½" (15.2 x 21.6cm)
	2 rectangles	2½" x 6½" (6.4 x 16.5cm)
	2 rectangles	4½" x 17½" (11.4 x 44.5cm)
	2 rectangles	2½" x 13½" (6.4 x 34.3cm)
Fabric B	6 strips	1½" (3.8cm) x WOF
Fabric C	2 strips	1½" x 22" (3.8 x 55.9cm)
Fabric D	2 strips	1½" x 22" (3.8 x 55.9cm)
Fabric E	2 strips	1½" x 22" (3.8 x 55.9cm)
Fabric F	1 rectangle	2½" x 24" (6.4 x 61cm)
	7 squares	2½" (6.4cm)

Tip
22" (55.9cm) is the full width of a fat quarter.

Fabric Colors

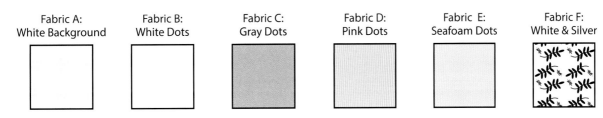

Fabric A:
White Background

Fabric B:
White Dots

Fabric C:
Gray Dots

Fabric D:
Pink Dots

Fabric E:
Seafoam Dots

Fabric F:
White & Silver

Quilt Construction

This quilt uses a slightly different approach from the basic steps shown in Lesson Four: How to Make a Picture Patchwork Quilt Top on page 18, but the same techniques apply.

1. Cut a 22" (55.9cm) length from one Fabric B strip and join it to one Fabric C strip along the long edge. Cut this combined strip into twelve 1½" (3.8cm) segments. Join these segments along the long edges to create a checkerboard strip.

2. Repeat Step 1 two more times to create a second and third checkerboard strip, then join all the strips together to create the top cake layer as shown on the quilt diagram. Set it aside.

3. Cut a 22" (55.9cm) length from one Fabric B strip and join it to one Fabric D strip along the long edge. Cut this combined strip into four 5" (12.7cm) segments. Repeat by cutting one additional Fabric B 22" (55.9cm) length and joining it to the remaining Fabric D strip. Cut a total of seven 5" (12.7cm) segments. Join these segments along the long edges so the colors alternate to create the second cake layer as shown on the quilt diagram. Set it aside.

4. Cut a 22" (55.9cm) length from one Fabric B strip and join it to one Fabric E strip along the long edge. Repeat with the remaining Fabric B strips and Fabric E strips. Cut these strips into ten 6" (15.2cm) segments. Join these segments along the long edges so the colors alternate to create the third cake layer as shown on the quilt diagram. Set it aside.

I appliquéd white lace and pink organza "icing" flowers on top of my cake, but you could also decorate it with embroidery or other decorative stitches.

5. Join two Fabric F squares and set them aside. Join the remaining five Fabric F squares in a row and set them aside.

6. On your design board or wall, arrange your 6½" x 36" (16.5 x 91.4cm) Fabric A rectangle into Row 1.

7. Arrange the 6½" x 12½" (16.5 x 31.8cm) Fabric A rectangles and the top cake layer into Row 2, consulting the quilt diagram for placement. Continue following the diagram.

8. Arrange the 5" x 11½" (12.7 x 29.2cm) Fabric A rectangles and the second cake layer into Row 3, consulting the quilt diagram for placement. Continue following the diagram.

9. Arrange the 6" x 8½" (15.2 x 21.6cm) Fabric A rectangles and the third cake layer into Row 4, consulting the quilt diagram for placement. Continue following the diagram.

10. Arrange the 2½" x 6½" (6.4 x 16.5cm) Fabric A rectangles and the Fabric F rectangle into Row 5, consulting the quilt diagram for placement. Continue following the diagram.

11. Arrange the 4½" x 17½" (11.4 x 44.5cm) Fabric A rectangles and the two Fabric F squares you joined in Step 5 into Row 6, consulting the quilt diagram for placement. Continue following the diagram.

12. Arrange the 2½" x 13½" (6.4 x 34.3cm) Fabric A rectangles and the five Fabric F squares you joined in Step 5 into Row 7, consulting the quilt diagram for placement. Continue following the diagram.

13. Arrange the remaining Fabric A rectangle into Row 8.

14. Collect the row pieces in order from left to right, turn over and label the wrong side of the last piece, and then clip them together until you're ready to sew.

15. Stitch the pieces in each horizontal row together, then carefully press the seams of each row in opposite directions.

16. Join the horizontal rows in numerical order from top to bottom to form the quilt center.

17. Carefully press the quilt top. I recommend pressing all the row seams toward the bottom of the quilt.

18. Optional: Add embellishments. I used appliqués of lace and pink organza to create a layer of icing on top. You could also add embroidery or decorative stitches.

19. Finish your quilt as desired.

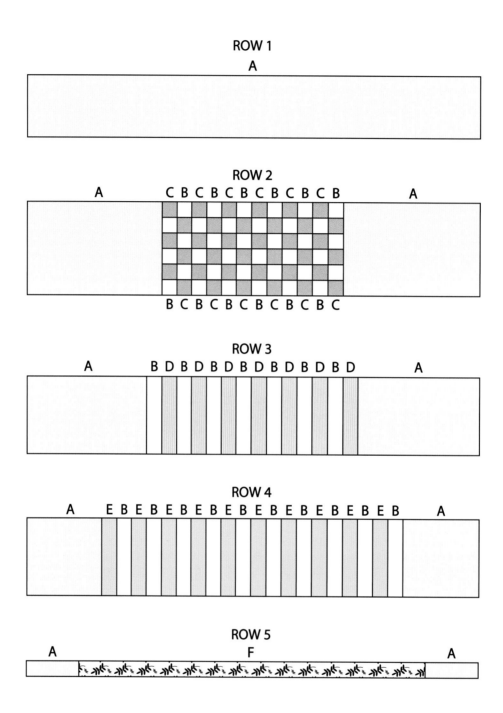

Detail: Rows 1–5

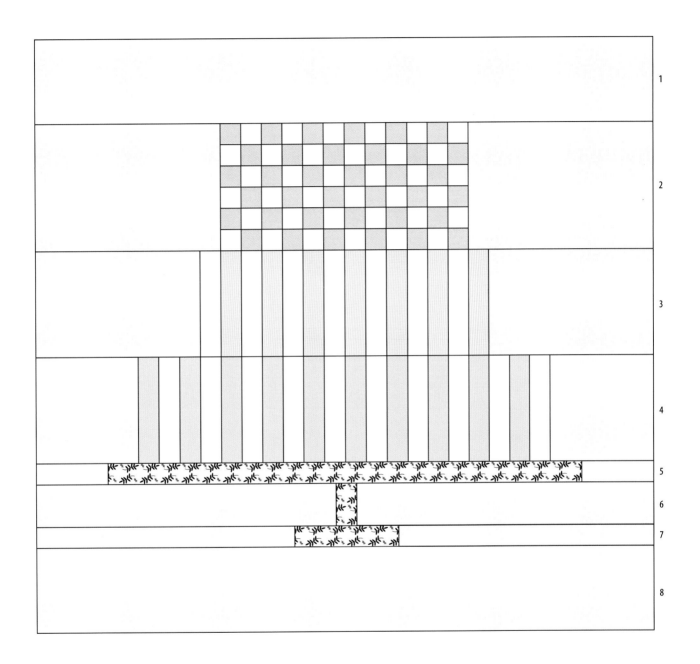

Quilt Diagram

I'm Lost

This overall design was inspired by a simple cross-stitch pattern I found online and reworked for fabric squares. My version includes a Mariner's Compass appliquéd on top to help the whale find his way, but the finished quilt looks great on its own. I created my Mariner's Compass with Robin Ruth's Strip-Pieced Mariner's Compass technique and ruler. It's the best method for making the most amazing and masterful compasses. Get more info at *www.robinruthdesign.com*.

Finished quilt measurements: 28" x 38" (71.1 x 96.5cm)

Fabric Requirements

Fabric A	¾ yd. (68.6cm)	white & blue dot print
Fabric B	8–10 fat quarters	assorted blue prints
Fabric C	½ yd. (45.7cm)	navy & light blue dot print
Fabric D	⅛ yd. (11.4cm)	midnight blue print

Cutting Instructions

Fabric A	157 squares	2" (5.1cm)
Fabric B	137 squares	2" (5.1cm)
Fabric C	6 squares	2" (5.1cm)
	3 strips	2" (5.1cm) x WOF
	1 strip	6" (15.2cm) x WOF
Fabric D	22 squares	2" (5.1cm)

Fabric Colors

Fabric A:
White & Dots

Fabric B:
Assorted Blues

Fabric C:
Navy Blue & Dots

Fabric D:
Midnight Blue & Dots

Quilt Construction

You will join 23 squares across 14 rows. Consult Lesson Four: How to Make a Picture Patchwork Quilt Top on page 18 as needed.

1. On your design board or wall, arrange your Fabric A and Fabric B squares into Rows 1 through 8, consulting the quilt diagram for placement.

2. On Row 9, add the whale's eye (a Fabric D square), consulting the quilt diagram for placement. Continue following the diagram.

3. Starting on Row 13, introduce the remaining Fabric D squares, consulting the quilt diagram for placement. Continue following the diagram.

4. On Row 14, introduce the Fabric C squares, consulting the quilt diagram for placement. Continue following the diagram until all the squares in this central section are placed.

5. Collect the squares in order from left to right, turn over and label the wrong side of the last square, and then clip them together until you're ready to sew.

6. Stitch the units in each horizontal row together, then carefully press the seams of each row in opposite directions.

7. Join the horizontal rows in numerical order from top to bottom to form the quilt center.

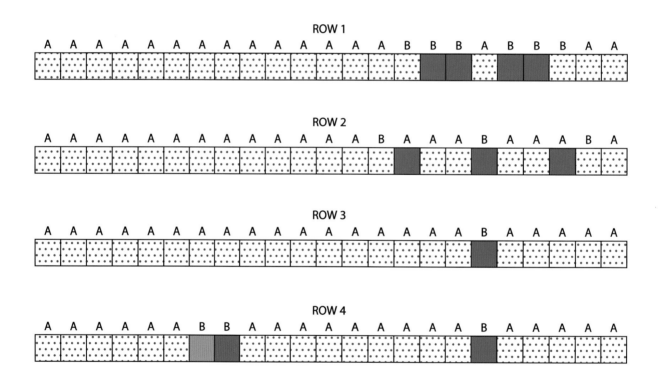

Detail: Rows 1–4

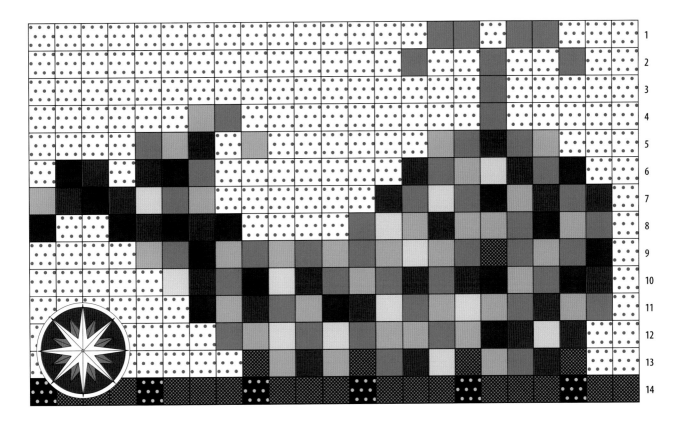

Quilt Diagram

8. Carefully press the quilt top. I recommend pressing all the row seams toward the bottom of the quilt.

9. Add the 2" (5.1cm) Fabric C border strips to the left and right edges of the quilt and then to the top edge.

10. Add the remaining Fabric C border strip to the bottom edge.

11. Press all the border seams away from the quilt center. Optional: Create and appliqué the Mariner's Compass on top as shown in the diagram.

12. Finish your quilt as desired.

Linked Blocks

While searching for inspiration, I saw many designs that were blocks . . . just blocks. Some were linked, layered, or overlapped, but I still thought they were a bit boring. I decided to make my version and ended up creating this striking bed runner—something I never thought I would make. In the end, I was surprised; it's become one of my favorite picture patchwork designs.

Finished quilt measurements: 28″ x 96″ (71.1cm x 2.4m)

Fabric Requirements

Fabric A	1 yd. (91.4cm)	white & blue dot print
Fabric B	⅝ yd. (57.2cm)	purple floral print
Fabric C	½ yd. (45.7cm)	blue floral print
Fabric D	⅝ yd. (57.2cm)	blue stripe print

Cutting Instructions

Fabric A	159 squares	3″ (7.6cm)
Fabric B	86 squares	3″ (7.6cm)
Fabric C	70 squares	3″ (7.6cm)
Fabric D	6 strips	3½″ (8.9cm) x WOF

Fabric Colors

Fabric A:
White & Blue Dots

Fabric B:
Purple Floral

Fabric C:
Blue Floral

Fabric D:
Blue Stripes

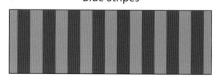

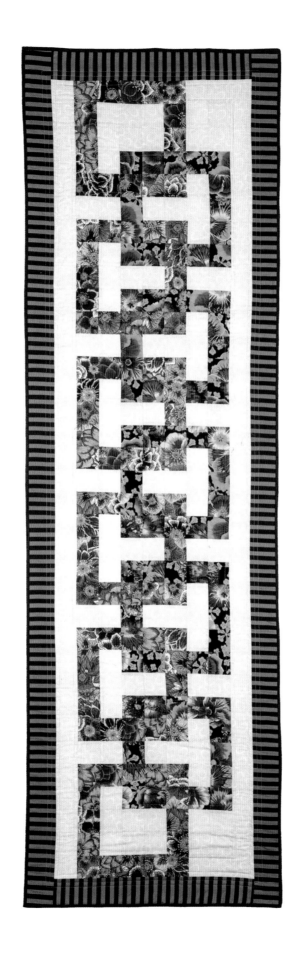

Quilt Construction

You will join 35 squares across 9 rows.
Consult Lesson Four: How to Make a Picture Patchwork
Quilt Top on page 18 as needed.

1. On your design board or wall, arrange your Fabric A squares into Row 1.

2. Starting on Row 2, introduce Fabric B squares, consulting the quilt diagram for placement. Continue following the diagram.

3. Starting on Row 4, introduce Fabric C squares, consulting the quilt diagram for placement. Continue following the diagram until all the squares in this central section are placed.

4. Collect the squares in order from left to right, turn over and label the wrong side of the last square, and then clip them together until you're ready to sew.

5. Stitch the units in each horizontal row together, then carefully press the seams of each row in opposite directions.

6. Join the horizontal rows in numerical order from top to bottom to form the quilt center.

7. Carefully press the quilt top. I recommend pressing all the row seams toward the bottom of the quilt.

8. Join the Fabric D border strips together, then cut this larger strip to match the right and left edge measurements of the quilt. Add the Fabric D border strips to the left and right edges of the quilt. Repeat to add Fabric D border strips to the top and bottom edges.

9. Press all the border seams away from the quilt center.

10. Finish your quilt as desired.

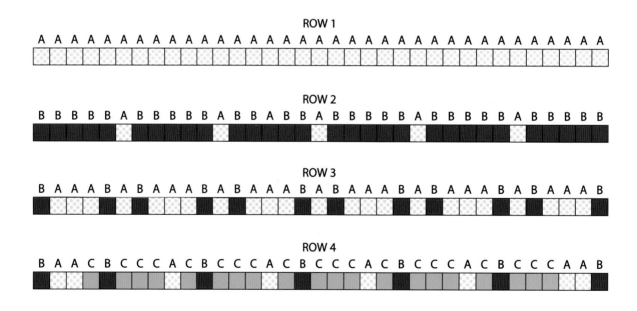

Detail: Rows 1–4

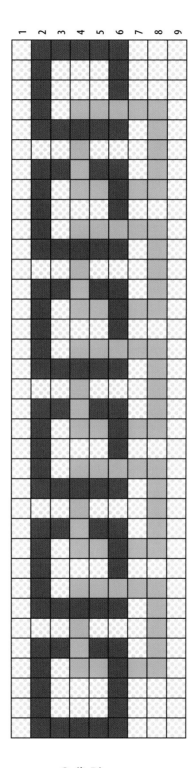

Quilt Diagram

L Is for . . .

Letters are a fun way to personalize a quilt for everyone you know. Choose a letter that tells a story, highlights a favorite memory, or just shouts out who they are. Initials are a way of giving someone a gift with a personalized touch—perfect for housewarming parties, baby showers, or weddings. I love to have my family's surname initial decorating our home as a reminder of who we are and the family we are a part of. The blocks in the center row of my initial are improv pieced blocks made by a special friend (Nancy Roberto) that I cut to fit to create a truly original piece. See pages 68–69 for additional letter and number designs.

Finished quilt measurements: 30" x 52" (76.2cm x 1.3m)

Fabric Requirements

Fabric A	1⅜ yd. (1.3m)	white & multicolor dot print
Fabric B	½ yd. (45.7cm)	purple & white dot print
Fabric C	assorted ⅛ yd. (11.4cm) pieces	assorted multicolor prints
Fabric D	¼ yd. (22.9cm)	purple stripe print
Fabric E	¾ yd. (68.6cm)	green grid print

Cutting Instructions

Fabric A	119 squares	4" (10.2cm)
Fabric B	39 squares	4" (10.2cm)
Fabric C	12 squares	4" (10.2cm)
Fabric D	6 strips	1" (2.5cm) x WOF
Fabric E	7 strips	5" (12.7cm) x WOF

Fabric Colors

Fabric A: White & Multicolor Dots	Fabric B: Purple & White Dots	Fabric C: Assorted Multicolor	Fabric D: Purple Stripes	Fabric E: Green Grid

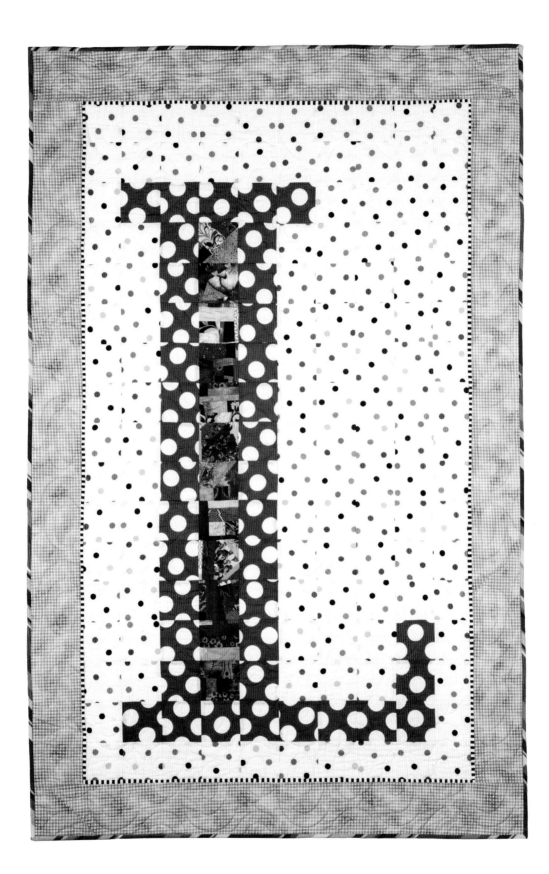

Quilt Construction

You will join 10 squares across 17 rows.
Consult Lesson Four: How to Make a Picture Patchwork
Quilt Top on page 18 as needed.

1. On your design board or wall, arrange your Fabric A squares into Rows 1 and 2.

2. Starting on Row 3, introduce Fabric B squares, consulting the quilt diagram for placement. Continue following the diagram.

3. Starting on Row 4, introduce Fabric C squares, consulting the quilt diagram for placement. Continue following the diagram until all the squares in this central section are placed.

4. Collect the squares in order from left to right, turn over and label the wrong side of the last square, and then clip them together until you're ready to sew.

6. Stitch the units in each horizontal row together, then carefully press the seams of each row in opposite directions.

7. Join the horizontal rows in numerical order from top to bottom to form the quilt center.

8. Carefully press the quilt top. I recommend pressing all the row seams toward the bottom of the quilt.

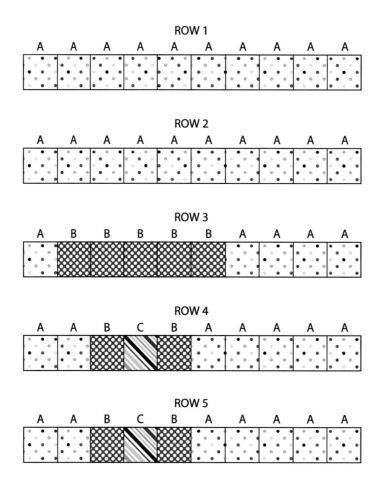

Detail: Rows 1–5

9. Press the Fabric D strips in half lengthwise, then join them on diagonals to create four flange strips that match the edge measurements of the quilt.

10. Add the Fabric D flange strips to the left and right edges of the quilt and then to the top and bottom edges.

11. Add the Fabric E border strips to the left and right edges of the quilt and then to the top and bottom edges.

12. Press all the border seams away from the quilt center.

13. Finish your quilt as desired.

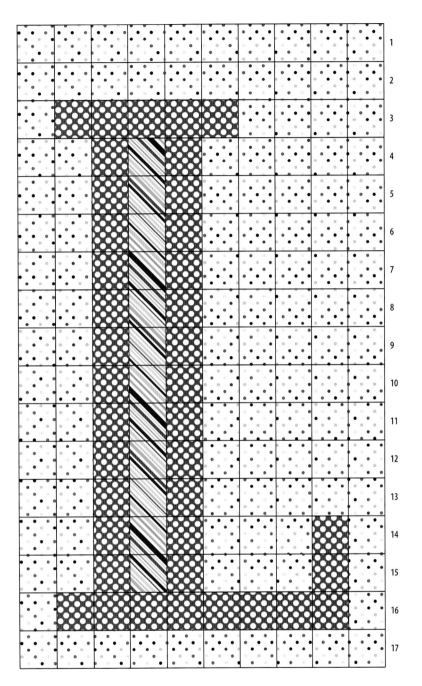

Quilt Diagram

Additional Letters and Numbers

The following letter and number designs are provided by Yarn Tree. For additional letter and number styles, see *yarntree.com*.

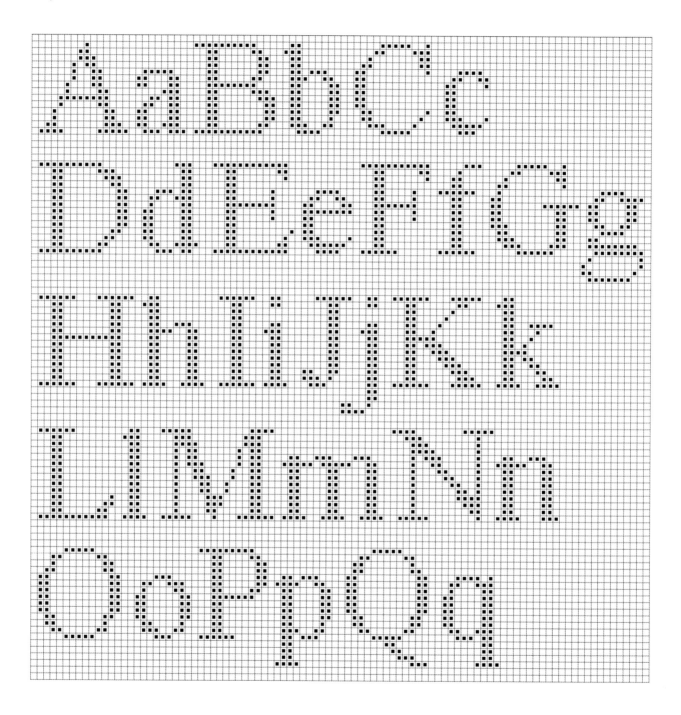

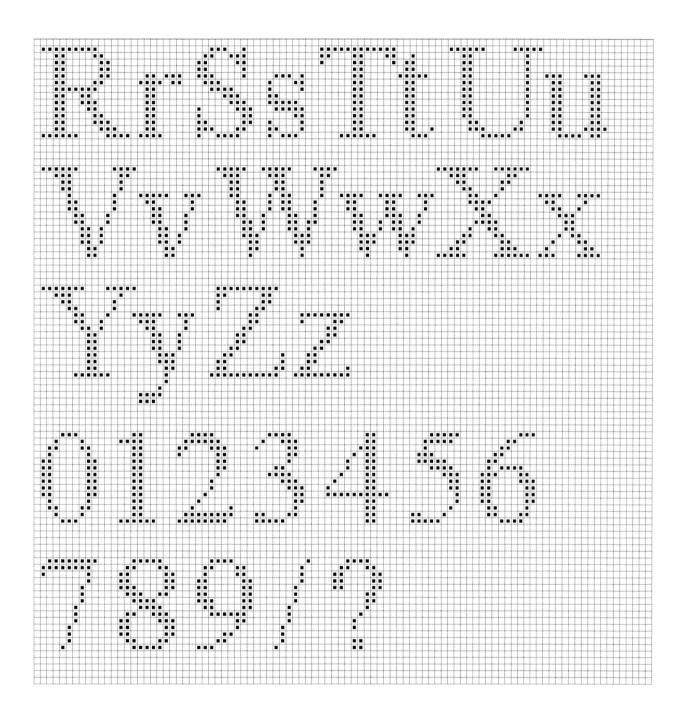

Lily Swan

This quilt is named for a swan I often see in a lily pond near my home. The finished piece uses different textures and intense free motion quilting for her feathers to create interest in the plain white swan. It also features an additional outer border created using the same picture patchwork technique used for the quilt center.

Finished quilt measurements: 72" x 64" (1.8 x 1.6m)

Fabric Requirements

Fabric A	½ yd. (45.7cm)	white on white print
Fabric B	2⅞ yds. (2.6m)	assorted blue prints
Fabric C	3" x 9" (7.6 x 22.9cm)	black print
Fabric D	3" x 6" (7.6 x 15.2cm)	orange solid
Fabric E	½ yd. (45.7cm)	tan solid

Cutting Instructions

Fabric A	231 squares	3" (7.6cm)
Fabric B	427 squares	3" (7.6cm)
Fabric C	3 squares	3" (7.6cm)
Fabric D	2 squares	3" (7.6cm)
Fabric E	6 strips	3" (7.6cm) x WOF

Fabric Colors

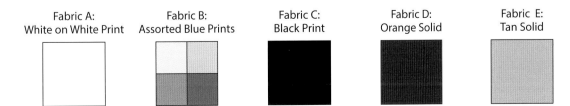

| Fabric A: | Fabric B: | Fabric C: | Fabric D: | Fabric E: |
| White on White Print | Assorted Blue Prints | Black Print | Orange Solid | Tan Solid |

Quilt Construction

You will join 25 squares across 22 rows.
Consult Lesson Four: How to Make a Picture Patchwork
Quilt Top on page 18 as needed.

1. On your design board or wall, arrange your Fabric B squares into Row 1.

2. Starting on Row 2, introduce Fabric A squares, consulting the quilt diagram for placement. Continue following the diagram.

3. Starting on Row 6, introduce Fabric C squares, consulting the quilt diagram for placement. Continue following the diagram.

4. Starting on Row 8, introduce Fabric D squares, consulting the quilt diagram for placement. Continue following the diagram until all the squares in this central section are placed.

5. Collect the squares in order from left to right, turn over and label the wrong side of the last square, and then clip them together until you're ready to sew.

6. Stitch the units in each horizontal row together, then carefully press the seams of each row in opposite directions.

7. Join the horizontal rows in numerical order from top to bottom to form the quilt center.

8. Carefully press the quilt top. I recommend pressing all the row seams toward the bottom of the quilt.

9. Join the Fabric E border strips together, then cut this larger strip to match the right and left edge measurements of the quilt. Add the Fabric E border strips to the left and right edges of the quilt. Repeat to add Fabric E border strips to the top and bottom edges.

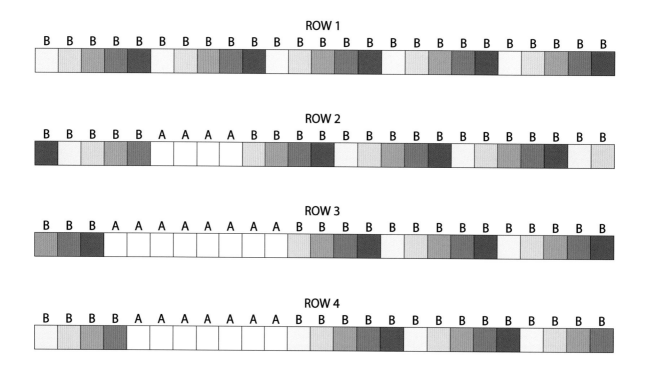

Detail: Rows 1–4

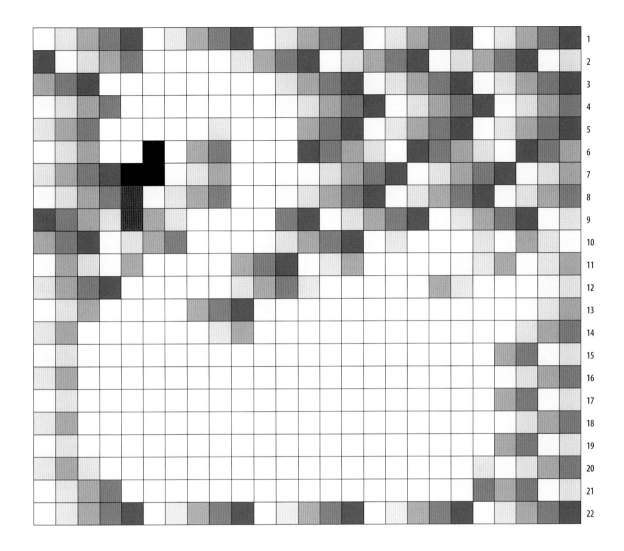

Quilt Diagram

10. Return the quilt top to the design board or wall. Join twenty-four 3" (7.6cm) Fabric B squares to create two separate strips. Add these strips to the left and right edges of the quilt.

11. Join twenty-nine 3" (7.6cm) Fabric B squares to create two separate strips. Add these strips to the top and bottom edges of the quilt.

12. Finish your quilt as desired.

Advanced Quilt Projects

Advanced doesn't always mean difficult—it often just means more complex. That's the case for the five quilts in this section. They use a larger number of squares, different sizes of squares and rectangles, and even some traditional pieced blocks and raw-edge appliqué. Each technique is still easily accomplished and fully illustrated within each design.

Pineapple Garden

Pineapples have always been a symbol of welcome and they remind me of a record my parents often played in the 1960s. This particular quilt features colorful flowers created by mixing floral fabric pieces. Make this quilt as a welcoming decoration to keep near your front door or as a reminder of your own fond memories of home. Welcome to my pineapple garden!

Finished Quilt Measurements: 49.5" x 74.5" (1.3 x 1.9m)

Fabric Requirements

Fabric A	1⅞ yds. (1.7m)	beige batik
Fabric B	1½ yds. (1.4m)	assorted green prints
Fabric C	1 yd. (91.4cm)	assorted light neutral prints
Fabric D	⅔ yd. (61cm)	assorted bright yellow prints
Fabric E	⅛ yd. (11.4cm)	orange print
Fabric F	1 yd. (91.4cm)	pansy floral print

Cutting Instructions

Fabric A	531 squares	2" (5.1cm)
Fabric B	361 squares	2" (5.1cm)
	2 strips	2" x 76½" (6.4cm x 1.9m)
Fabric C	235 squares	2" (5.1cm)
Fabric D	233 squares	2" (5.1cm)
Fabric E	14 squares	2" (5.1cm)
Fabric F	54 squares	2" (5.1cm)
	2 strips	5" x 76½" (12.7cm x 1.9m)

Fabric Colors

Fabric A: Beige Batik

Fabric B: Assorted Greens

Fabric C: Assorted Light Neutrals

Fabric D: Assorted Bright Yellows

Fabric E: Orange

Fabric F: Pansy Floral

Quilt Construction

You will join 28 squares across 51 rows.
Consult Lesson Four: How to Make a Picture Patchwork Quilt Top on page 18 as needed.

1. On your design board or wall, arrange your Fabric A and Fabric B squares into Rows 1 through 16, consulting the quilt diagram for placement.

2. Starting on Row 17, introduce Fabric C and Fabric D squares, consulting the quilt diagram for placement. Continue following the diagram.

3. Starting on Row 20, introduce Fabric E squares, consulting the quilt diagram for placement. Continue following the diagram.

4. Starting on Row 37, introduce the Fabric F squares to start building the patchwork flowers. Also begin adding more Fabric B squares, consulting the quilt diagram for the placement of both. Continue following the diagram until all the squares in this central section are placed.

5. Collect the squares in order from left to right, turn over and label the wrong side of the last square, and then clip them together until you're ready to sew.

6. Stitch the units in each horizontal row together, then carefully press the seams of each row in opposite directions.

7. Join the horizontal rows in numerical order from top to bottom to form the quilt center.

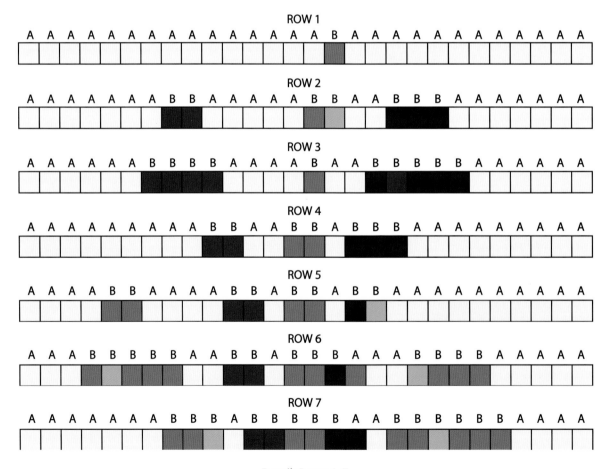

Detail: Rows 1–7

8. Carefully press the quilt top. I recommend pressing all the row seams toward the bottom of the quilt.

9. Join the Fabric B border strips together, then cut this larger strip to match the right edge measurement of the quilt. Add the Fabric B border strip to the right edge of the quilt.

10. Add the Fabric F border strip to the right edge of the Fabric B border in the same way.

11. Press all the border seams away from the quilt center.

12. Finish your quilt as desired.

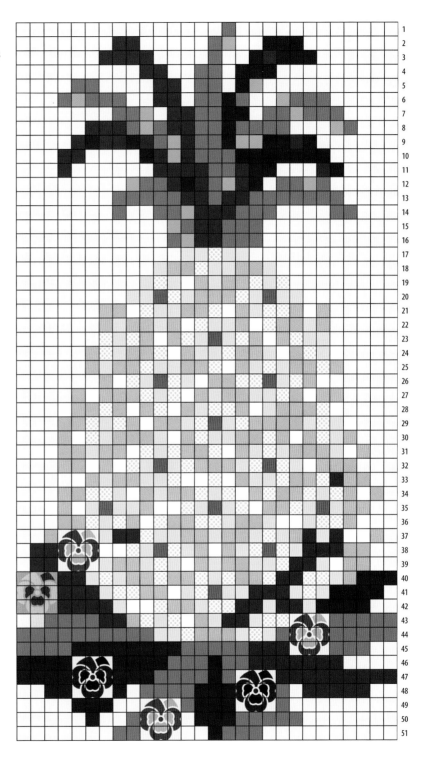

Quilt Diagram

Charted Heart Duo X 2

The Charted Heart Duo came from a what-if question. The original design was a single heart with Nine Patch blocks worked into the layout. But what if there were two hearts and hearts within those hearts? I decided that more is always better—and this design is the result.

Finished quilt measurements: 45" x 54" (1.1 x 1.4m)

Fabric Requirements

Fabric A	1½ yds. (1.4m)	black floral print
Fabric B	1 fat quarter	white starburst print
Fabric C	⅝ yds. (57.2cm)	black & white striped print
Fabric D	1 yd. (91.4cm)	large black & purple dot print
Fabric E	¾ yd.–1 yd. (68.6–91.4cm)	small black & purple dot print
Fabric F	½ yd. (45.7cm)	purple houndstooth print
Fabric G	¾ yd. (68.6cm)	purple agate print
Fabric H	¼ yd. (22.9cm)	blue pebble print
Fabric I	1 fat quarter	periwinkle starburst print

Cutting Instructions

Fabric A	74 squares	3½" (8.9cm)
	7 strips	1½" (3.8cm) x WOF
Fabric B	8 strips	1½" x 22" (3.8 x 55.9cm)
Fabric C	33 squares	3½" (8.9cm)
	6 strips	1½" (3.8cm) x WOF
Fabric D	7 strips	4½" (11.4cm) x WOF
Fabric E	27 squares	3½" (8.9cm)
Fabric F	8 squares	3½" (8.9cm)
Fabric G	19 squares	3½" (8.9cm)
Fabric H	23 squares	3½" (8.9cm)
Fabric I	8 strips	1½" (3.8cm) x WOF

Tip

22" (55.9cm) is the full width of a fat quarter.

Fabric Colors

Fabric A:
Black Floral

Fabric B:
White Starburst

Fabric C:
Black & White
Stripe

Fabric D:
Large Black &
Purple Dot

Fabric E:
Small Black &
Purple Dot

Fabric F:
Purple
Houndstooth

Fabric G:
Purple Agate

Fabric H:
Blue Pebble

Fabric I:
Periwinkle
Starburst

Make the Nine Patch Blocks

Make the following 3½" (8.9cm) Nine Patch blocks using these instructions.
- 32 Fabric A with Fabric B (labeled A/B on the detailed row illustration on page 83)
- 16 Fabric A with Fabric I (labeled A/I on the detailed row illustration on page 83)

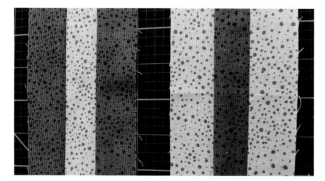

1. Sew one Fabric A strip (represented by light pink in the example photo) between two Fabric B or Fabric I strips (represented by dark pink in the example photos). Sew one Fabric B or Fabric I strip between two Fabric A strips. Press the combined strip units carefully, keeping the lines as straight as possible.

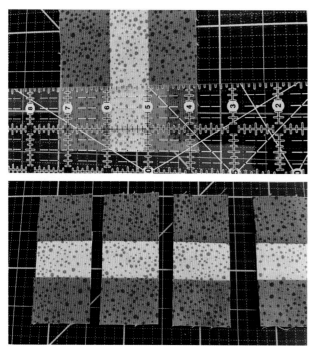

2. Cut the combined strip units into 1½" (3.8cm) segments.

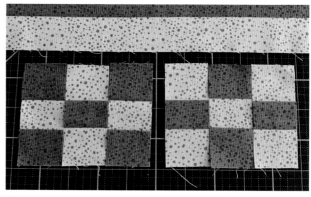

3. Arrange the cut strip sets to form Nine Patch blocks as shown.

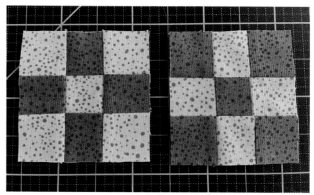

4. Sew each block together carefully, matching and butting the seams to achieve precise construction.

Quilt Construction

You will join 14 squares across 17 rows.
Consult Lesson Four: How to Make a Picture Patchwork Quilt Top on page 18 as needed.

1. On your design board or wall, arrange your Fabric G, Fabric E, Fabric C, Fabric H, Fabric A, and Fabric F squares into Rows 1 and 2, consulting the quilt diagram for placement.

2. Starting on Row 3, introduce Fabric A/B Nine Patch blocks, consulting the quilt diagram for placement. Continue following the diagram.

3. Starting on Row 4, introduce Fabric A/I Nine Patch blocks, consulting the quilt diagram for placement. Continue following the diagram until all the squares and pieced blocks in this central section are placed.

4. Collect the squares in order from left to right, turn over and label the wrong side of the last square, and then clip them together until you're ready to sew.

5. Stitch the units in each horizontal row together, then carefully press the seams of each row in opposite directions.

6. Join the horizontal rows in numerical order from top to bottom to form the quilt center.

7. Carefully press the quilt top. I recommend pressing all the row seams toward the bottom of the quilt.

8. Join the Fabric C border strips together, then cut this larger strip to match the right and left edge measurements of the quilt. Add the Fabric C border strips to the left and right edges of the quilt. Repeat to add Fabric C border strips to the top and bottom edges.

9. Add the Fabric D border strips to the Fabric C border in the same way.

10. Press all the border seams away from the quilt center.

11. Finish your quilt as desired.

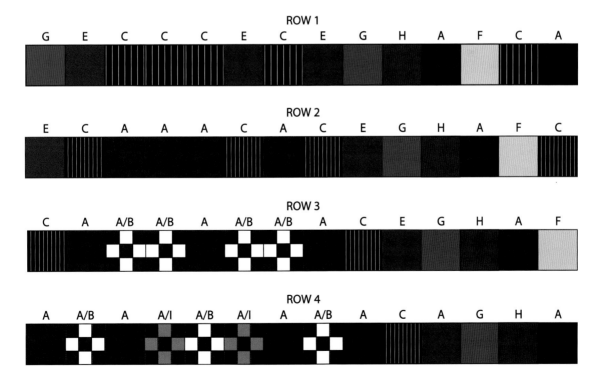

Detail: Rows 1–4

Quilt Diagram

The Nine Patch blocks create a hearts-within-hearts design that makes this quilt top a mix of beautiful statement piece and subtle home accent.

Pedal and Petals

Pedaling around with a basket full of petals seems like a relaxing way to spend an afternoon. This project is the perfect design to decorate a summer beach house and maybe even nap under after a leisurely ride along your favorite bike path. For the background, I've cut strips and squares of different sizes to help cut down on the weight and more easily create straight edges.

Finished quilt measurements: 50½" x 41½" (1.3 x 1.1m)

Fabric Requirements

Fabric A	3¼ yds. (3m)	green on green neutral print
Fabric B	½ yd. (45.7cm)	dark gray dot print
Fabric C	⅞ yd. (80cm)	taupe and silver print
Fabric D	½ yd. (45.7cm)	teal and silver print
Fabric E	⅛ yd. (11.4cm)	purple dot print
Fabric F	5" x 7" (12.7 x 17.8cm)	silver pebble print
Fabric G	⅛ yd. (11.4cm)	gold pebble print
Fabric H, optional	assorted scraps	assorted floral prints

Cutting Instructions

Fabric A	31 squares	5½" (14cm)
	358 squares	1½" (3.8cm)
	6 strips	1½" x 4½" (3.8 x 11.4cm)
	4 strips	1½" x 5½" (3.8 x 14cm)
	3 strips	1½" x 6½" (3.8 x 16.5cm)
	7 strips	1½" x 7½" (3.8 x 19.1cm)
	1 strip	1½" x 8½" (3.8 x 21.6cm)
	1 strip	1½" x 10½" (3.8 x 26.7cm)
	1 strip	1½" x 11½" (3.8 x 29.2cm)
	3 strips	1½" x 12½" (3.8 x 31.8cm)
	1 strip	1½" x 14½" (3.8 x 36.8cm)
	1 strip	1½" x 15½" (3.8 x 39.5cm)
	1 strip	1½" x 22½" (3.8 x 57.2cm)

Continued on page 88.

Precut-friendly design!
Use 1½" (3.8cm) skinny strip rolls.

Fabric Colors

Fabric A:
Green on Green
Neutral

Fabric B:
Dark Gray Dots

Fabric C:
Taupe Silver

Fabric D:
Teal Silver

Fabric E:
Purple Dots

Fabric F:
Silver Pebble

Fabric G:
Gold Pebble

Fabric B	160 squares	1½" (3.8cm)
Fabric C	318 squares	1½" (3.8cm)
Fabric D	159 squares	1½" (3.8cm)
Fabric E	46 squares	1½" (3.8cm)
Fabric F	3 squares	1½" (3.8cm)
Fabric G	26 squares	1½" (3.8cm)
Fabric H, optional	assorted floral appliqué pieces	preferred size

Quilt Construction

For the bicycle itself, you will join 46 squares across 32 rows. The background is formed of larger strips and squares. This quilt uses a slightly different approach from the basic steps shown in Lesson Four: How to Make a Picture Patchwork Quilt Top on page 18, but the same techniques apply.

1. On your design board or wall, arrange your 1½" (3.8cm) Fabric A and Fabric E squares into Rows 1 through 3, consulting the quilt diagram for placement.

2. Starting on Row 4, introduce Fabric D and Fabric G squares, consulting the quilt diagram for placement. Continue following the diagram, leaving space for the larger squares and strips that will be added later.

3. Starting on Row 14, introduce Fabric B squares, consulting the quilt diagram for placement. Continue following the diagram.

4. Starting on Row 16, introduce Fabric C squares, consulting the quilt diagram for placement. Continue following the diagram.

5. Starting on Row 23, introduce Fabric F squares, consulting the quilt diagram for placement. Continue following the diagram until all the squares in the bicycle are placed.

6. Add ten 5½" (14cm) Fabric A squares each across the top and bottom bicycle rows. Then add the remaining 11 large squares around the bicycle as shown in the diagram.

7. Add the 15½" (39.5cm) Fabric A strip above the bicycle seat, the three 12½" (31.8cm) Fabric A strips below the bicycle basket, and the 11½" (29.2cm) Fabric A strip below those three.

8. Place Fabric A strips to the left of the bicycle tire rows in the following order top to bottom: Rows 16 and 29 = 7½" (19.1cm); Rows 17 and 28 = 6½" (16.5cm); Rows 18–19 and 26–27 = 5½" (14cm); Rows 20–25 = 4½" (11.4cm); and Row 30 = 8½" (21.6cm).

9. Add the remaining Fabric A strips to Row 31 as shown in the diagram to finish filling in the design.

10. Starting with Rows 1–5, collect the bicycle squares in order from left to right, turn over and label the wrong side of the last square, and then clip them together until you're ready to sew.

11. Stitch the squares in Rows 1–5 together, then carefully press the seams of each row in opposite directions. Join these horizontal rows in numerical order from top to bottom, then place the section back on your design board or wall.

12. Repeat Steps 10 and 11 in sections. Join the bike seat rows and the Fabric A strip above them. Join the Rows 6–10 and the Fabric A strip at the end of Row 10. Join Rows 11–15, excluding only the large Fabric A square on the left side. Finally, join all remaining bicycle rows, including all Fabric A strips.

13. Stitch the top and bottom rows of Fabric A squares together. Stitch the Fabric A squares together on either side of the completed bicycle handlebar section. Stitch the Fabric A squares to the left of the bicycle seat section and between the bicycle seat section and the basket section. Stitch the final Fabric A square to the remaining incomplete section. You should now have six horizontal sections. Carefully press the seams of each section in opposite directions.

14. Join the horizontal sections in order from top to bottom to form the quilt center.

15. Carefully press the quilt top. I recommend pressing all the row seams toward the bottom of the quilt.

16. **Optional:** Add embellishments. I used fusible appliqués techniques to add flowers to the basket. You could also add silk flowers after finishing.

17. Finish your quilt as desired.

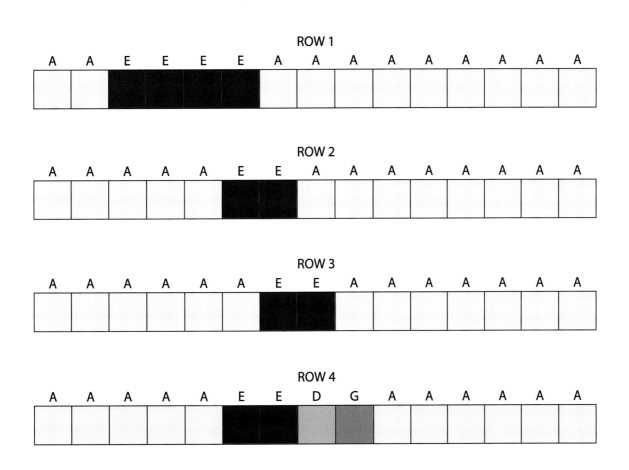

Detail: Bicycle Rows 1–4

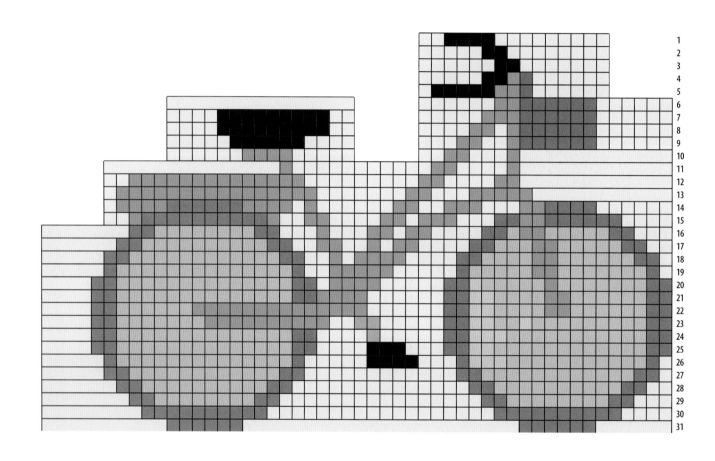

Quilt Diagram—Bicycle Rows

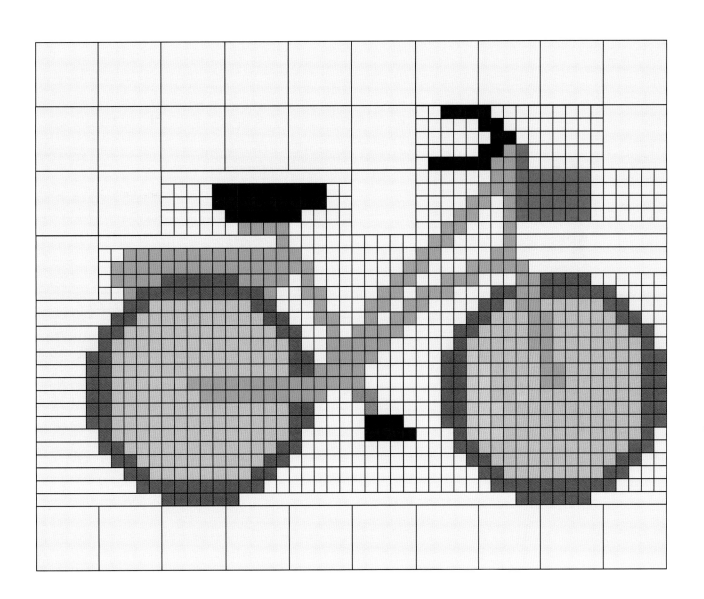

Full Quilt Diagram

See Step 13 on page 89 for instructions
for filling in the larger Fabric A blocks.

Skyline Evergreen

Skyline Evergreen is my name for the tree I see out my living room window. It was planted a few years ago to replace a giant evergreen that had fallen. I have always wanted to decorate it with lights and ornaments, but my homeowners' association would not look kindly upon my efforts. I've interpreted my vision in fabric instead! This quilt uses Nine Patch and Sawtooth Star blocks, but you can simplify the design by using single-fabric squares of the same size.

Finished quilt measurements: 45" x 47" (1.1 x 1.2m)

Fabric Requirements

Fabric A	½ yd. (45.7cm)	silver print
Fabric B	½ yd. (45.7cm)	silver pebble print
Fabric C	½ yd. (45.7cm)	gold pebble print
Fabric D	6–10 fat quarters	assorted green prints
Fabric E	¼ yd. (22.9cm)	red pebble print
Fabric F	½ yd. (45.7cm)	silver and gold starburst print

Cutting Instructions

Fabric A	35 squares	3½" (8.9cm)
	4 squares, for Sawtooth Star block	1¼" (3.2cm)
	1 square, for Sawtooth Star block	4" (10.2cm)
Fabric B	17 squares	3½" (8.9cm)
	3 strips	1½" (3.8cm) x WOF
	2 squares, for Sawtooth Star blocks	2" (5.1cm)
	8 squares, for Sawtooth Star blocks	1¼" (3.2cm)
Fabric C	23 squares	3½" (8.9cm)
	3 strips	1½" (3.8cm) x WOF
	3 squares, for Sawtooth Star blocks	2" (5.1cm)
	12 squares, for Sawtooth Star blocks	1¼" (3.2cm)
Fabric D	46 squares	3½" (8.9cm)
	12 strips	1½" x 22" (3.8 x 55.9cm)

Tip

22" (55.9cm) is the full width of a fat quarter.

Continued on page 94.

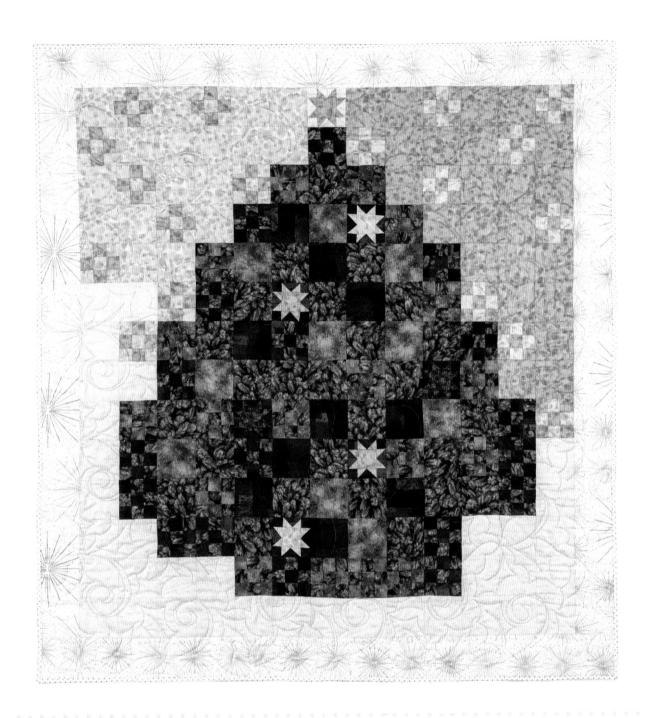

Fabric Colors

Fabric A:
Silver

Fabric B:
Silver Pebble

Fabric C:
Gold Pebble

Fabric D:
Assorted Greens

Fabric E:
Red Pebble

Fabric F:
Silver/Gold Starburst

	24 squares, for Sawtooth Star blocks	1¼" (3.2cm)
	6 squares, for Sawtooth Star blocks	4" (10.2cm)
Fabric E	2 squares, for Sawtooth Star blocks	2" (5.1cm)
	8 squares, for Sawtooth Star blocks	1¼" (3.2cm)
Fabric F	5 strips	3½" (8.9cm) x WOF

Make the Nine Patch Blocks

Make the following Nine Patch blocks. Refer to page 82 for the Nine Patch block instructions.
- 9 Fabric B with Fabric C (labeled B/C on the detailed row illustration on page 96)
- 9 Fabric C with Fabric B (labeled C/B on the detailed row illustration on page 96)
- 36 Fabric D, mixing light and dark shades (labeled D on the detailed row illustration on page 96)

Make the Sawtooth Star Blocks

Make the following 3½" (8.9cm) Sawtooth Star blocks using these instructions. **Note:** This square-based technique was developed from Lazy Girl's Flying Geese Ruler.
- 1 Fabric A with Fabric C (labeled A/C on the detailed row illustration on page 96)
- 2 Fabric D with Fabric B (labeled D/B on the detailed row illustration on page 96)
- 2 Fabric D with Fabric C
- 2 Fabric D with Fabric E

1. Draw a diagonal line from corner to corner on the wrong sides of four 1¼" (3.2cm) Fabric C, Fabric B, or Fabric E squares (represented by floral fabric in the example photos). Place two of these squares marked sides up on the corners of a 4" (10.2cm) Fabric A or Fabric D square (represented by pink dotted fabric in the example photos). The marked line should extend from the upper right to the lower left corner. Sew on both sides of the marked line.

2. Cut along the marked line to create two separate units.

3. Press both units open. Place one each of the remaining marked squares marked sides up on the tips of the larger triangles as shown in the bottom example.

4. Sew on both sides of the marked line on each piece. Then cut along the marked lines on each piece to create four separate units.

5. Press the units open. **Note:** These units are called flying geese.

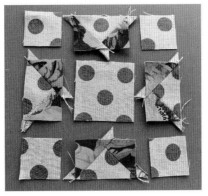

6. Place your center 2" (5.1cm) Fabric C, Fabric B, or Fabric E square. **Note:** *In this example, my center square matches the polka dot fabric rather than the floral fabric. Your finished squares will be the opposite—the central stars will all be the same fabric.* Position a flying geese unit on each side with their points toward the center as shown. Place a 1¼" (3.2cm) Fabric A or Fabric D square at each corner.

7. Stitch the units into three rows, then press the seams in opposite directions in each row as shown.

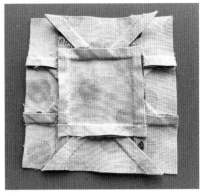

8. Join the rows and press the seams outward as shown.

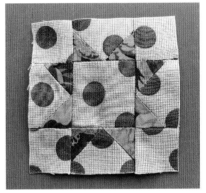

9. You will need to square the finished Sawtooth Star block to the correct measurements.

Quilt Construction

You will join 13 squares across 14 rows.
Consult Lesson Four: How to Make a Picture Patchwork
Quilt Top on page 18 as needed.

1. On your design board or wall, arrange your Fabric B and Fabric C squares, your B/C and C/B Nine Patch blocks, and your A/C Sawtooth Star block into Row 1, consulting the quilt diagram for placement.

2. Starting on Row 2, introduce Fabric D Nine Patch blocks, consulting the quilt diagram for placement. Continue following the diagram.

3. Starting on Row 3, introduce Fabric D squares, consulting the quilt diagram for placement. Continue following the diagram.

4. Starting on Row 4, introduce D/B Sawtooth Star blocks, consulting the quilt diagram for placement. Continue following the diagram.

5. Starting on Row 6, introduce Fabric A squares and D/C Sawtooth Star blocks, consulting the quilt diagram for placement. Continue following the diagram.

6. Starting on Row 8, introduce D/E Sawtooth Star blocks, consulting the quilt diagram for placement. Continue following the diagram until all the squares and pieced blocks in this central section are placed.

7. Collect the squares in order from left to right, turn over and label the wrong side of the last square, and then clip them together until you're ready to sew.

8. Stitch the units in each horizontal row together, then carefully press the seams of each row in opposite directions.

9. Join the horizontal rows in numerical order from top to bottom to form the quilt center.

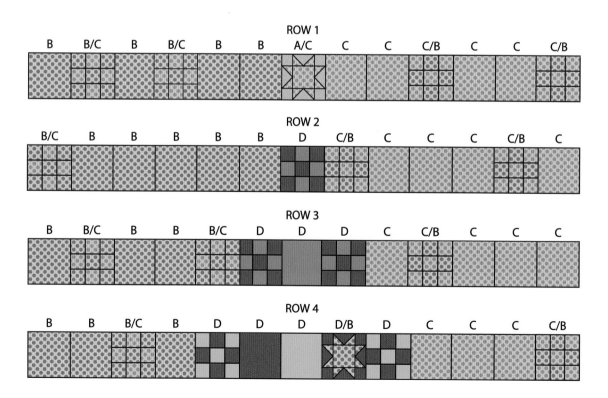

Detail: Rows 1–4

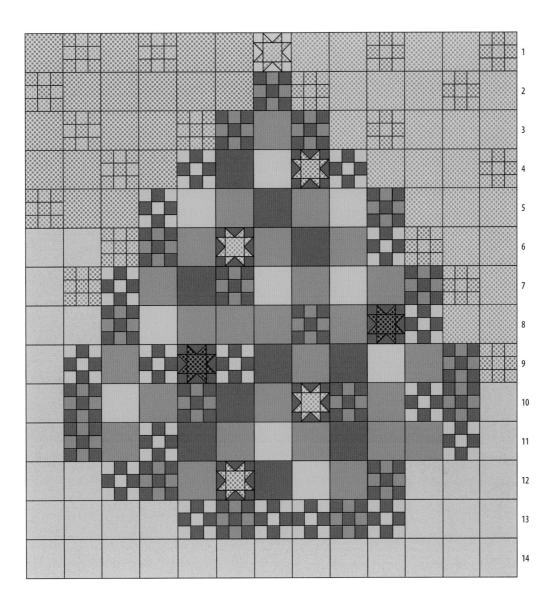

Quilt Diagram

10. Carefully press the quilt top. I recommend pressing all the row seams toward the bottom of the quilt.

11. Measure the left and right edges of the quilt and cut two Fabric F strips to size. Add the Fabric F border strips to the left and right edges of the quilt.

12. Measure the top and bottom edges of the quilt with the left and right border strips included and cut two Fabric F strips to size. Add the Fabric F border strips to the top and bottom edges of the quilt.

13. Press all the border seams away from the quilt center.

14. Finish your quilt as desired.

Stitching Away

The only design I absolutely knew I could not leave out is a classic sewing machine. I can't even remember not having a machine to sew on. I used my mother's until I was 14 years old when I was gifted a brand-new machine by a family member who was moving away and couldn't take it with her. I was thrilled! This quilt is my thank-you to Aunt Jennie for the hours of pleasure that machine brought me. This quilt includes Sawtooth Star blocks and some longer strips of fabric, but you can replace both with smaller squares if you want to simplify your finished piece.

Finished quilt measurements: 42″ x 63″ (1.1 x 1.6m)

Fabric Requirements

Fabric A	1½ yd. (1.4m)	neutral dot print
Fabric B	1 yd. (91.4cm)	assorted black tonal prints
Fabric C	⅛ yd. (11.4cm)	magenta floral print
Fabric D	assorted ⅛ yd. (11.4cm) pieces	assorted floral prints
Fabric E	⅛ yd. (11.4cm)	white solid for Sawtooth Star blocks
Fabric F	⅜ yd. (34.3cm)	magenta pebble print
Fabric G	⅝ yd. (57.2cm)	multicolor stripe

Cutting Instructions

Fabric A	507 squares	2″ (5.1cm)
Fabric B	315 squares	2″ (5.1cm)
Fabric C	1 strip	2″ x 29½″ (5.1 x 74.9cm)
Fabric D	46 squares	2″ (5.1cm)
	7 squares, for Sawtooth Star blocks	2″ (5.1cm)
	28 squares, for Sawtooth Star blocks	1¼″ x 2″ (3.2 x 5.1cm)
Fabric E	7 squares, for Sawtooth Star blocks	4″ (10.2cm)
	28 squares, for Sawtooth Star blocks	1¼″ (3.2cm)
Fabric F	5 strips	2″ (5.1cm) x WOF
Fabric G	4 squares	2″ (5.1cm)
	6 strips	3½″ (8.9cm) x WOF

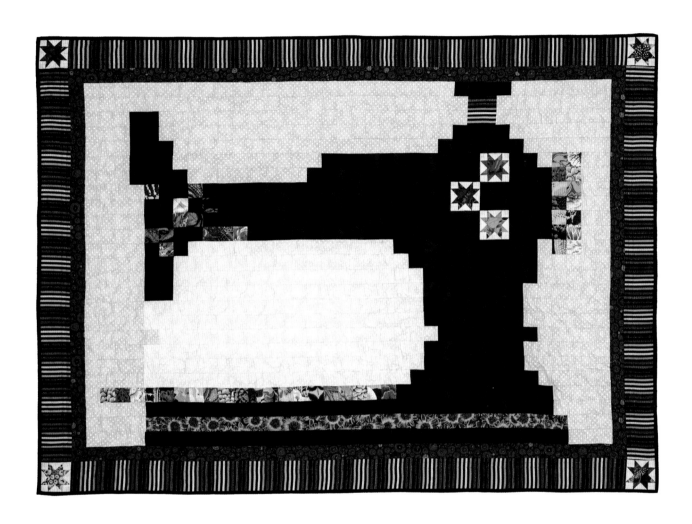

Fabric Colors

Fabric A:
Neutral Dots

Fabric B:
Assorted Black
Tonals

Fabric C:
Magenta Floral

Fabric D:
Assorted Florals

Fabric E:
White Solid
(in Sawtooth Star
Blocks)

Fabric F:
Magenta Pebble

Fabric G:
Multicolor Stripe

Make the Sawtooth Star Blocks

Make the following 3½" (8.9cm) Sawtooth Star blocks. Refer to page 94 for the Sawtooth Star block instructions.
• 7 Fabric E with matching pieces of Fabric D

Quilt Construction

You will join 37 squares across 25 rows.
Consult Lesson Four: How to Make a Picture Patchwork Quilt Top on page 18 as needed.

1. On your design board or wall, arrange your Fabric A and Fabric B squares into Row 1, consulting the quilt diagram for placement.

2. Starting on Row 2, introduce Fabric G squares, consulting the quilt diagram for placement. Continue following the diagram.

3. Starting on Row 6, introduce Fabric D squares and the Sawtooth Star blocks, consulting the quilt diagram for placement. **Note:** The Sawtooth Star blocks will fill two rows and two columns. Continue following the diagram.

4. On Row 24, introduce the Fabric C strip, consulting the quilt diagram for placement. Continue following the diagram until all squares in this central section are placed.

5. Collect the squares in order from left to right, turn over and label the wrong side of the last square, and then clip them together until you're ready to sew. **Note:** The Sawtooth Star blocks will be stacked within two rows.

6. Stitch the units in each horizontal row together, then carefully press the seams of each row in opposite

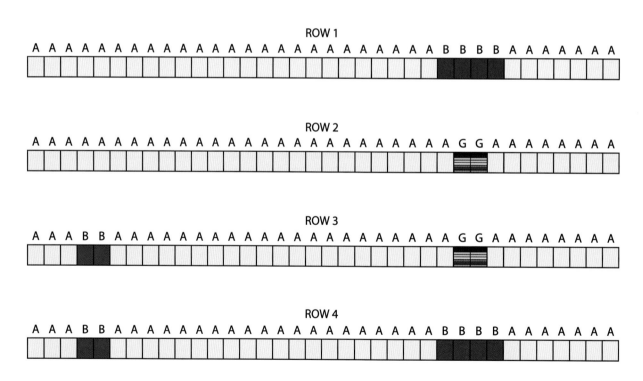

Detail: Rows 1–4

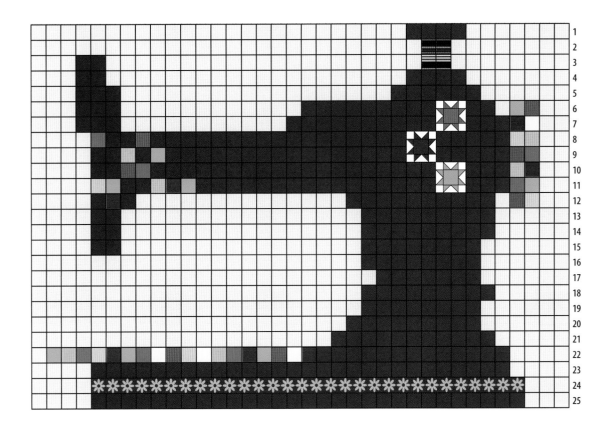

Quilt Diagram

directions. **Note:** For the six rows that include Sawtooth Star blocks, join the squares on either side of the blocks as you normally would, then join these row sections together along their long edges. Once you've created these joined two-row pieces, add them on either side of the Sawtooth Star blocks to finish the horizontal two-row units. Connect them to the other horizontal rows as usual.

7. Join the horizontal rows in numerical order from top to bottom to form the quilt center.

8. Carefully press the quilt top. I recommend pressing all the row seams toward the bottom of the quilt.

9. Join the Fabric F border strips together, then cut this larger strip to match the right and left edge measurements of the quilt. Add the Fabric F border

strips to the left and right edges of the quilt. Repeat to add Fabric F border strips to the top and bottom edges.

10. Join the Fabric G border strips together, then cut this larger strip into four strips matching the edge measurements of the quilt. Add the shorter Fabric G border strips to the left and right edges of the Fabric F border.

11. Join a Sawtooth Star block to each end of the top and bottom Fabric G border strips. Add these pieced border strips to the top and bottom edges of the quilt.

12. Press all the border seams away from the quilt center.

13. Finish your quilt as desired.

Index

Acknowledgments

First, "thanks" does not express enough the gratitude I owe to my BFF in every way, Patricia Ross Conover, for her support, editing skills, and so much more.

I owe a huge thank you, as well, to Joyce Hengy Hughes for sharing her room with me at MAQ and encouraging me to take this plunge, to Mary Diamond for her generous long arm services and weekly tea visits, and to Mary Nesnay for pulling me back from the illustration ledge.

Also, to FreeSpirit Fabrics, thank you for the very, very generous donation of the Kaffe Fassett Collective fabrics that inspired many of the designs you see here. I am a KAFFE-AHOLIC!

To Amelia and the team at Fox Chapel, thanks for taking a big chance on a newbie.

I have always been someone who was not afraid to jump in headfirst without knowing how to swim—and all of you have kept me from drowning.

And finally, I have had the pleasure, opportunity, and blessing to have been surrounded by so many exceptional quilting friends, supporters, students, shop owners, guilds, Facebook friends, and more. How do I thank all the wonderful people who put up with me day to day? Each of you have made me who I am and are a part of this book. Naming all of you would require too many pages. You know who you are, so, to every one of you I say, "thank you." I will always be grateful.

Dedication

This book is dedicated to my husband of 47 years, Anthony Gennaro Lepore. There are no words to express his commitment, love, and support for me and everything I do. Without him, this book would never have been written and I would not be who I am today. When you see him with me at events, be sure to thank him for all that he has done.

About the Author

"Where Do I Begin?" is part of the title of a song that most will not recall, but to me it means so much. It's the theme song from *Love Story*, the very first movie my husband of 47 years took me to (back when we were first dating). We went to the opening showing in 1970 in New York City (I am a Jersey girl, after all). This is part of where my love story begins.

Tony (my husband), fabric of any kind, and a sewing machine are the pieces that make up my life. Tony is, of course, my first love, but fabric truly creates passion and excitement in my life. For nearly 30 years I was the owner of a gift and decorative accessory wholesale company. But things change and so did I. Owning a business is a lot more work and a lot less glamour than I'd hoped for! All of the importing, travel, accounting, and other worries took its toll.

I have sewed and created fabric projects since the age of 7. In the early 1980s, while operating my wholesale company, I was introduced to quilting. I began teaching quilting classes around the same time. I was quickly hooked.

In the early 2000s, I began to create quilts for competition and publication. I loved doing both! My work has been published, exhibited at national and regional quilt shows, and was even featured as a special exhibit at the International Quilt Festival in Houston, Texas. (And, yes, there have been a few ribbons won.)

In 2022, I joined the faculty of the annual Mid-Appalachian Quilters educational seminar and discovered that my work might be suitable for a book! With no idea what was to come, I submitted a proposal. This book and the designs included are the result and they are what drives me. I truly love what I do.

And that's my lifelong love story: with Tony, with fabric, and with my sewing machine. Sharing my passion for fabric and quilting is another special chapter in that story.